CHAPTER ONE
- THE AGM

It had all started when the ball landed in that vat of Stilton and Blacky had run off with the money. My captaincy skills had been put to the test that day, but I think that I had passed with flying colours, well maybe not everyone thought so. Anyway, I digress, let me tell you my story.

'Bing or maybe it was ping,' whatever it was, that was the noise that my computer made when the email arrived. It was headed 'Important: Cricket Club – AGM,' and I opened it with maniacal haste to make sure that I was free on the prescribed date, which I would be, unless Jane, my understanding wife of 15 or maybe 16 seasons, I mean years, had booked a trip to see her mother and needed me to manage our three kids. But I had honed my mother-in-law avoidance strategies to near perfection over the years and so was confident that I would be able to attend the meeting.

'Jane, darling,' I added the latter for effect, 'it's that time again, it's AGM time.' I may have sung the last bit through my sheer delight.

I feel that I need to explain the purpose of an Annual General Meeting. It is an opportunity for members of cricket clubs up and down the country to whip off their winter coats and announce to all and sundry that the cricket season was officially open for business. The meeting is monotonous to the extreme, but its arrival is generally met with excitement by club members as it heralds that the season is only a few months away.

"Barry, every year we go through this charade. It starts by you telling me that it's AGM time and that you have never missed one, that you won't get drunk and stagger home smelling of kebabs and then, to make matters worse, I have to listen to you banging on about it the next day.'

'Ok cool, so that's a yes then, I will add it to my calendar.'

Jane rolled her eyes and went back to making the tea, muttering something about her mother being right all along and why hadn't she listened.

A key area of interest that brings the masses to the AGM is the election of the team captains. I had been first team captain of Buntingford Smedley

ANY GIVEN SATURDAY

A Buntingford Smedley Cricket Club Story

Sanjay Murthy

Como House Ltd

Copyright © 2025 Sanjay Murthy

ISBN-13: 9798289189189

Cover design by: Sanjay Murthy

Printed in the United Kingdom

*This book, and everything that I do, is
to show my beautiful wife that I can
combine dreaming with action.*

Cricket Club for the last three seasons, overseen two consecutive promotions and fully expected to be re-elected to the post. In preparation for this inevitability, I opened a new Word document on my laptop and wrote in capital letters 'STRUCTURE, ACCOUNTABILITY, DISCIPLINE, FOCUS, UNITY, CRICKET – BY BARRY BRIGGS, FIRST XI CAPTAIN,' adding this to summon the universal energy that Jane had once told me existed.

I rolled my neck from side to side in preparation for this important piece of work and started to write down my thoughts, dreams, selections and tactics with which Buntingford Smedley's first team would enjoy success.

I had already thought about how I wanted us to conduct ourselves and play this year. In fact I had spent much of the winter thinking about this and now I needed to get these musings down onto paper.

I started off with writing and underlining the word 'training' and decided that Tuesday night, when we also selected the teams for the forthcoming matches would be good, as that I could have a close look at who is on form before making my choices. I obviously enjoyed the first choice of players whilst the captains of the seconds and thirds could then pick whoever I left on the shelf, as it were. Training, I noted, was also compulsory and I wrote down 'no practice, no playing' and wondered if I should ask one of my design team at the small agency that I owned to create a poster, print it out and pin it to the noticeboard in the pavilion.

Deciding that was probably a bit officious and

someone would either deface it or rip it down, I had just started to write about The Wreck, our ground, when I was sidetracked by lamenting that we used to have a midweek and a Sunday team too, but as with a lot of these things, interest dwindled and otherwise keen cricketers were forced to assist in domesticity or worse still, visit relatives in neighbouring shires to discuss their shrubberies and, somewhat ironically, the state of the national cricket team.

I shook my head and focused on thinking how to make The Wreck our stronghold and ensure that we stayed unbeaten there throughout the year. I decided that this would be achievable by showing the right attitude from the moment that we arrived up to the moment that we left.

Fully into my flow now, I hammered the keyboard into submission with my edicts on what time I expected the team to arrive before the match, that warming up had to be outside of the bar and partaking in throw downs and light fielding drills was compulsory. This, I deduced, would show the opposition that we were a force to be taken seriously.

And it was in this vein that the document continued with tactics for the match day including gems that I had heard from current international captains on the TV such as 'try and win the toss' and 'bat first and bat long.' I made sure that I included these in my opus.

I was about to start the section on how I wanted my bowlers to perform when I heard Jane shouting that tea was ready. I admit that I mulled over replying that I needed to finish my work first but knew that this would be met with some choice language, so I locked the screen in case of a cyber security leakage and went to join the family.

I was deep in thought as to how I could bring about the downfall of Pillingsbury CC, who as well as being our local rivals, were also promoted with us last season, when I took my place at the table to be greeted by the backs of the digital tablets of my three children.

'How was your day guys?'

Silence ensued.

I was about to try again when tea arrived as announced and the conversation, whilst slow at first, did start and soon turned to cricket and the upcoming AGM.

'Are you captain again this year, dad?' beamed Ben, aged 12 who had his eye on the top job in later years, maybe after he had finished captaining England.

'I am son,' I replied maybe prematurely, 'big year this year as I reckon we could go up again, but we need to keep the best team on the field.'

'Daddy, if the players are not on the field you would lose,' volunteered Ella aged 7 going on 16, adding as an afterthought, 'unless you were batting then of course only two of you would be on the field'.

Josh, who displayed middle child syndrome, responded with a cackle and leaned back in his chair. There was a proclamation coming, as there usually was with him, but as he was about to let forth his views on girls and their knowledge of cricket, he overbalanced and fell arse over cobblers onto the floor. Jane leapt like the proverbial salmon and ran around the table to make sure her favourite, not that she would admit it, was all right and not physically damaged in any way. Thankfully, Josh had landed on his arse and not his cobblers, so all was well and, when the laughing had subdued, I turned to my daughter to explain that it was just a turn of phrase. However, the moment was gone as she was engrossed in asking Ben whether the girl in year 8 was his girlfriend or not.

I awoke with rare vigour on the morning of the AGM, and after dropping the kids off at school, I drove the short distance to my small design company. The crew was already at their desks when I arrived.

'Morning, morning, 'how were your weekends?' I enquired cheerily.

After a brief discussion on the beer-worthy merits of the two local pubs in the village and why a Taj Mahal special was the best way to end a Saturday night, an opinion that I could not disagree with, I plonked myself down at my desk and opened the Word document, which now had an acronym - SADFUC.

Over the last few weeks, I had researched how other captains would approach a new season and had tweaked the manifesto, adding points on team discipline, tactics, bonding role plays and culture. I had stumbled on an essay in The Wisden Magazine, a publication I considered essential reading for cricket addicts, which suggested that successful captains were always thinking about scoring rates for each phase of the game, whether batters were to walk or not and what level of sledging would be permitted.

For those of you who are unfamiliar with cricket, I will provide a brief explanation. Those who play the sport on a weekend are experts at watching and critiquing the professionals, who have spent their lives perfecting their craft. The amateurs then take this behaviour to their everyday lives and inflict it on the innocent bystanders with whom they cross bats on a Saturday. So 'to walk or not' means, if you hit it and get caught by the wicketkeeper you are required to stand like a plum, waiting for the umpire to give you out. If the umpire does indeed end your innings with a deft raising of their index finger, then the expected behaviour is to look at them with disdain, shake your head, mutter something about spectacles, question their parental lineage and complain all over again in the changing room. You may be lucky and find yourself reprieved by a short-sighted umpire, if so, the correct behaviour is to remain at the crease looking smug whilst the opposition question the legality of your birth.

Sledging is swearing with very occasional comedy thrown in.

I decided to create a dossier on each of the players that I wanted in my first team squad. I gave each player his own page with his name, picture, nickname and role in the team. Below this I wrote a few lines on their abilities and personality followed by an analysis on their respective strengths, weaknesses, opportunity to perform and threats to their place in the team.

'Right let's start with the opening batters,' I thought.

Greg 'Flash' Stevens - RH (right hand) Batsman

Greg is cocky, flamboyant, thinks he is a maverick match-winner and rarely is. He thinks his main role is to get Gilo out as quickly as possible.

S: Technically good, drives well, solid defence

W: Can't play off his legs, erratic runner

O: Take leg stump guard and drive through cover

T: Bowling on his legs, LBW candidate, Gilo

Alfie "Gilo" Aikens - LH Batsman

Lovable lummox – loyal, oblivious, speaks before he thinks. Loves a beer and this is the key to getting the best out of him. Make sure the beer is post-match.

S: Strong but impulsive

W: Impulsive but strong

O: Get a few runs early and tee off

T: The other batters

I find that it is always important to know whether a batter is left or right-handed because you need to know who to borrow kit from when you have forgotten yours again. Apart from a box, a vital piece of plastic that protects your chinchillas from the impact of the cricket ball, which you should never borrow regardless of which hand you use. I remember, and I get hot sweats when I do, the time a ball me in the nether regions. I collapsed on all fours with a squeal, whilst the opposition and the rest of my team laughed like there is no tomorrow, which I certainly felt may come true. After what seemed like a week, I rose gingerly, removed said item to ensure the plastic had not split, reinserted it, and awaited the next ball whilst my stomach was flipping pancakes.

I continued in this vein, building up a picture of each of my intended squad, whilst occasionally fielding pesky questions from members of my design team. Soon my plans for the season were in place and all I had to do was to have them ratified by the club chair, Colin 'The Badger" Campbell. Oh, and be re-elected as skipper.

'The MCC would be proud of this document,' I thought as I leaned back in my chair and, after twiddling my thumbs for five minutes wondering whether to email it to their committee, I decided that it was time for lunch.

If you didn't know, the MCC is an acronym of the Marylebone Cricket Club, the custodians of the laws of the game. New memberships are rare and generally have been passed down through generations of the same families. The requirement of a member is to wear bacon and egg-coloured jackets and ties, applaud politely when a batsman enters or leaves the field of play and never join in the Mexican Wave, which is an annoying waste of time that happens when the game is dull. People all around you stand up, wave their sweaty armpits in your face, obstruct your view and boo loudly at those who don't partake, like the MCC members.

The afternoon progressed slowly with colleagues asking for guidance on designs, clients giving us new projects and paying on time. But I simply yearned for 7:30 pm when I would turn up at The Wreck, order a pint of bitter and hope that there was no opposition for my nomination as first team captain. I said as much to one of our designers, who I suspected may be a decent bowler given his height and build.

'AGM tonight,' I started, having walked the length of the office with the pretext of inspecting his work.

'Oh yeh'

'Yeh, should be the first's captain again.'

'Oh yeh'

'Yeh, three promotions in a row,' and with that I held up three fingers to accentuate my point.

'Oh yeh'

'Yeh and I have been writing a manifesto to help the team achieve an unprecedented fourth.'

'Oh yeh, he monotoned, adding, to my surprise, 'what's it called?'

'SADFUC,' I replied.

I think that I heard muffled laughter from the other designers, but I had already popped over to see Sheila from Accounts about my expenses.

My workday finally came to an end and, as I left, the design team wished me luck at the AGM. I thanked them graciously, not noticing the smirks on their faces, and arrived home about 6pm to see the kids doing their homework whilst inhaling what looked like Turkey Twizzlers and oven chips.

I mentally scanned the SADFUC document to see if I had written a section on diet and nutrition. All I remember writing was that it was forbidden to be part of any pub lock-in on a Friday night and to have a carbohydrate-rich breakfast. Neither of these currently applied so I stole one of Ben's chips and went to seek out Jane.

'Hey ho,' I said jauntily, 'you know what tonight is don't you?'

'Yes Baz, you have marked the days off on the calendar since that bloody email.'

'Woohoo,' I cried, kissed her on the cheek, practiced a forward defensive shot and went to join the nosebagging.

After I had wolfed down a red-hot jacket potato oozing with melted cheddar and last night's reheated chilli, scalding my tongue in the process, I asked the kids how their day had been, avoided any prolonged response, and skipped upstairs to change into my AGM attire, which consisted of freshly pressed jeans and matching shirt, into which I slipped before donning my clean, non-gym trainers and the crowning glory, my new cricket jumper that Jane had knitted for the upcoming season.

I looked in the mirror and inspected my reflection, club crest sitting proudly on one breast with the year of the season and my initials embroidered on the sleeve. I vowed that I would win the league this season in recognition of Jane's knitting efforts. She would like that I thought and practiced a few imaginary shots before taking a deep breath and walking down the stairs of my own private pavilion.

I had secretly hoped that Jane and the kids would be lined up at the bottom of the stairs as I walked past, wishing me well, all the best and what not, but they were all in the lounge watching Love Island. So, I opened the front door devoid of applause and marched to my chariot. Ten minutes later I had arrived at The Wreck and, after parking next to a newish blue Volvo, I entered the pavilion to be greeted by a great crescendo of emptiness.

Well, that isn't entirely correct as there was an occupant of the bar-cum-tearoom, and that was Colin 'The Badger Campbell, our chair and local dignitary. He came from a lengthy line of local Campbells, who were originally farmers until a descendent in the 1700s decided that brewing would be a better option. He built a factory and turned the local wheat into beer, thus starting an empire that has lasted until this day. The Badger was the managing director and then chair, thus accumulating bucket loads of both wealth and status.

'Hello there Barry', said The Badger, 'bit early aren't we?'

'Uhh, hi Badger, no 7:30 it said on the email, and well it's that now, right?' I was a bit confused at the lack of bodies.

'Ahh balls up there, I got the date wrong you see, I said Tuesday but then realised that Paul had arranged the bowls club for AGM tonight so I moved it to tomorrow. I sent an email, I think.'

Paul aka Noodle was The Badger's brother, third team captain and the club secretary. He was given his nickname on account of him being tall, thin, pasty looking and generally slimy. No one really liked him as he was a nasty piece of work and lived in his brother's shadow. He too had once worked at the brewery but was dismissed for some creative book keeping and diversion of funds.

'Shouldn't you be at that AGM then?' I asked.

'Well technically yes, but to be honest, I couldn't face two AGMs in one week, I mean they are frightfully dull, aren't they?'

I had to agree, but was still confused as to why I hadn't seen this mystery email.

'I don't remember any email Badg, I can't believe that I would have missed it.'

I then added, 'What are you doing here anyway?'

'Well, you know, stock-take, tidying up, that sort of malarkey' responded The Badger, 'tell you the truth the missus, was watching that bloody Love Island and I had to get out. Such rubbish TV we have now. Fancy a pint as you're here, or are you a Love Islander too?'

'No, I'll have a beer with you, we can go through my plans for the first team this season.'

'If elected old boy, if elected' countered the bluff old

cove.

I looked around the bar-cum-tearoom imagining my end of season victory speech, whilst The Badger poured a pint of ale, threw away half as it was all foam, blamed the taps, the lines and plonked a dubious glass of murky brown liquid down in front of me.

'Have that on me' he said, poured himself a perfect pint, totted up the amount owed and walked away to the other side of the bar muttering that he would 'pay later as he had no change you see.'

In the meantime, I had set my laptop on a small bar table and opened the PowerPoint presentation. Ahh yes, I had forgotten to tell you that I had created this beauty in lieu of the previous document. I proceeded to run The Badger through my plans for the season, showing him who would do what, the support they needed and how I intended to make the club renowned in the locality.

How true that last statement would become.

Two hours and four pints later I had finished, and The Badger leaned back and pronounced that Buntingford Smedley CC was indeed in safe hands and that they should all be proud to be associated with me, one Barry Compton Briggs.

An hour later and a bit worse for wear, I stumbled elatedly into the taxi that I had wisely booked when The Badger suggested that another beer was required. After a pit stop at Kebab Korner I fell out of the cab and into my lounge.

'S'tomorrow,' I tried.

The kids had gone to bed, Love Island had borne both its soul and other bodily parts to the nation and Jane was knitting a cricket jumper for Ben to wear to his U13 match.

'What is?'

'AGM, s'tomorrow. The Badger said he sent an email, but hic..I didn't get it,' I slurred indignantly

'Let's hope you remember what days you are meant to be playing.'

Despite being five pints to the good, I declined to engage in my wife's attempts to bait me and instead slumped down next to her, dislodging her knitting basket and dispatching its contents on to the floor.

'Oh for pity's sake Barry, go to bed' she instructed.

Not wanting to fall foul of my chief campaign manager, I duly got up, at the third attempt, and sloped off, not before practising a deft leg glance in front of the hallway mirror and falling over the strategically positioned side table, smashing a small vase into three large pieces.

I felt a bit delicate the next morning, five pints and a kebab on a school night is never a clever idea but I also had a pain in my midriff and wondered if it had been caused by my table incident the previous evening.

'Ooohh my ribs hurt,' I winced.

'That'll teach you for keeping me awake by farting and snoring all night.'

I was considering a response when she added, 'muttering Bradman's average in your sleep is tantamount to asking for a smack in the mouth in addition to the dig in the ribs.'

Rather than having the desired effect, it reminded me that the AGM was actually tonight and that I needed to amend my presentation in light of The Badger's advice. I voiced this thought to Jane and promptly wished that I hadn't bothered.

Eager to escape her withering look and the imminent verbal put down, I ambled off to have a shower and, with humanity re-entering my being, I dressed and went downstairs to find the kids in the midst of breakfast chaos, with tablets playing different programs, breakfast cereal strewn across the table and each in various stages of being dressed. Ella, for example, had decided that today she would be wearing tights and no skirt to school, and Josh had gelled his hair to the point of no return.

I surveyed the scene as I popped some bread into the toaster. It will soon be the cricket season and maybe, just maybe, Ben would captain his age group again and the other two children would show the slightest inclination to play the world's greatest sport. This glorious daydream was interrupted by Ella pulling the tablecloth off the table as she got down, resulting in various breakfast paraphernalia cascading onto the floor.

'Oh Ella, for Pete's sake why are you so clumsy all of the time?' I shouted through a mouth full of buttered toast.

The other two sat back revelling in their sister's discomfort but they weren't going to escape my hungover wrath that easily. I suggested that they were far from perfect and that they could also have created this mess, resulting in mock outrage from the boys.

Jane silently entered the scene and, with hands on hips, suggested that I should take them to school and leave her to bring order back to the homestead.

'Come on you troublesome bunch,' I said suddenly all fatherly, cuffing Josh playfully on the back of his head, dislodging a lump of gel, and heralded them out to the drive to find that my car was missing. Memories of five pints and a kebab produced a slight feeling of nausea and a realisation that it was still at The Wreck.

Having negotiated the use of Jane's car and convincing her that I was under the legal alcohol limit to drive, I dropped the brood off and arrived at the office, ready to make the required alterations to my presentation.

I had simultaneous feelings of deja vue and fear at 7:30pm that evening when my taxi pulled into the Buntingford Smedley CC car park. The only two vehicles parked there were mine and The Badger's Volvo and I wondered whether it had been there all night. I straightened my jumper, pushed my blond hair to one side, thinking that it needed a trim before the season started, paid the cabbie and walked towards the clubhouse.

Taking a deep breath in lieu of the ridicule I was about to face given yesterday's episode, I walked into the bar-cum-tearoom that made up the vast majority of the 1970s building that served as the headquarters for both the Buntingford Smedley cricket and football teams.

'Evening all' I said in greeting to The Badger, who hadn't been there all night and had in fact driven home, and to Noodle, his brother, who was charm personified.

I hear you got the wrong day, you pillock.'

I threw him a pitiful look and muttered.

'Well, I didn't see the email and anyway how can sodding bowls be more important than cricket.'

With him told, I bought a round of drinks and wandered over to chat with the club treasurer, keen to avoid any further interactions with anyone who preferred bowls.

I soon heard cars rolling down the drive, doors slamming shut and voices growing cheerier and louder as various club members arrived and made their way into the pavilion. After various 'how-dos', 'did you winter well', 'big season ahead and 'oh I am sorry to hear that', the members of Buntingford Smedley CC were called to attention and asked to take their places in readiness for the chair's introduction, election of club officials and a few traditional post-AGM drinks to congratulate those who had successfully lobbied their way into power. I had hoped that would be me.

'Seats, gentlemen,' shouted The Badger, 'let's get started then.'

'And lady,' rebuked the club treasurer.

'Quite, quite, and lady, remiss of me.'

'Welcome all old, and new members to the Buntingford Smedley Cricket Club Annual General Meeting,' he started, leaving the assembled to wonder who these mysterious new members could be and where they were hiding.

'This is your club remember and we, the committee, are here for you at any time of the season. You will always find my door open and I will be creating a chair's corner, in that area of the bar for that very purpose,' and with that he dramatically flung his arm to indicate where this would be located, leaving the crowd to guess whether there would be an actual door or not, whilst grumbling that it was all a waste of time, causing Noodle to shush them in deference to his brother.

'We have a lot to get through tonight, so let's have some decorum,' instructed the club chair and continued 'item one, proposed increase in match fees from £4 to £5.'

This was a bad start to proceedings and the crowd let the committee know by emitting a universal groan and utterances about some people not paying their bar bill.

Most vociferous in this department was Darren 'Dazzler' Perkins, the first team's star bowler who strengthened his on-pitch stamina with off-pitch lethargy and was without any known occupation.

'A fiver Badger, you need pay your bar bills, then we don't have to cough up more cash like' he accused.

'How do you have any money to pay for a drink anyway Darren,' asked Noodle in support of his brother, 'you're horizontal on your sofa most of the day.'

'I work you old sod and at least I can actually play cricket, you just pretend that you can and only get to captain the thirds 'cos you're Badg's brother.'

Noodle was about to retort with another demeaning comment when I decided that I needed to intervene in case things got out of control and fisticuffs erupted.

'Shut it you pair of tits or we'll be here all night.'

The crowd oohed and generally murmured their approval of my interjection and so The Badger, after nodding his thanks, continued.

'Item two, an increase in bar prices.'

This AGM was very much like the twenty or so I had previously attended and continued with as much efficiency as you can expect when 30, mainly men, gather in a room drinking cold beer. There were various agenda items that needed the arbitrary proposer, seconder and a show of hands to carry the motion into the statute books.

'And now we come to item number seven,' continued The Badger, 'the time honoured, and may I say hugely important, preparation of the teas.

If you don't already know about the cricketing tea, then let me enlighten you. The reputation of a club in the local cricketing community rests on the quality of the tea that it produces for consumption by the two teams, umpires and general hangers-on in the mid-innings break.

'I propose the motion,' continued The Badger, 'that the responsibility for creating these teas is shared between all the members of the three teams on a rota basis, rather than the current situation of just the captains' wives making them. I think we should put this to the vote, so could I see a show of hands of those who agree?'

The human mind is a cunning devil which assesses each situation considering whether it will mean more work for it or not. If you are an average weekend player, your Saturday mornings are consumed by just two things, whether your kit is clean and what time you need to be at the meeting point.

I was lucky in that I had a wife who understood that my playing whites needed to be washed, ironed and neatly folded in my wardrobe awaiting both my inspection and acceptance. Like a Shakespearian actor smuggling into his costume and assuming the character, cricketers with clean whites transform themselves into an international player.

However, the reality is that most cricketers spend Saturday morning trying to find their kit and I too have been in that situation, normally when Jane takes the kids to see her parents for the weekend. Horror descends upon me, when I realise that it is still in its bag, which may be in my car or worse, at the club, swearing blindly that I thought I had washed it, realising that I did not know how the washing machine worked, going into a blind panic as to whether to go and buy new whites or scrub the grass stains off in the sink, and finally deciding that ironed dirty whites are better than creased ones. So now armed with pressed, but dirty whites, I can now spend some time thinking about my afternoon performance and what liquid rewards my feats would bring. What I do not have the mental or physical capacity for is making the tea.

Jane, apart from being the doyenne of clean kits, is also willing to make the tea and so I could delegate this important task, safe in the knowledge that tray after tray of sandwiches, scones and assorted supermarket snacks would arrive and that I could take all the credit. A lot of the cricketing fraternity however did not have this luxury and would do anything to palm their responsibility off to someone else. Hence the voting on article seven was split very much along the lines of those who have and those who have not.

'Ahh, a tied vote and I, as chair, have the casting one,' proclaimed The Badger, after counting the show of hands

Upon such matters does the lifeblood of a cricket club exist and it takes a tough and uncompromising leader to make the final ruling. Unfortunately for us, we had The Badger.

'I have considered the matter and have decided that last year's tea making policy will remain,' adding with a nervous laugh, 'and that I will have to deal with the wife when I get home.'

And it was in this vein that we continued, with breaks for comfort and refreshment slowing down an already snail-like process. I shuffled uncomfortably in my chair as I wanted to get to the important stage, but it wasn't until 10pm that the vote for the captains took place.

The third team captaincy was between Noodle and a younger player, who had the temerity to stand against the chair's brother in such a public arena. As most of the AGM members were first and second team players as well as club officials, they frankly didn't care enough for the lower tiers of the club, and they gave Noodle his head.

'And the third team skipper is Paul Campbell,' confirmed The Badger, upon which the newly re-elected captain rose to thank everyone, shook the upstart by the hand whilst deciding to drop him altogether from his team.

'And now a show of hands for the candidates for the captaincy of the second team, who are Tim 'Hawk' Kestrel and,' on turning the paper over, The Badger said, 'ahh, just Hawk then.'

The aforementioned Tim 'Hawk' Kestrel is my friend and a well-liked and a successful captain in his own mediocre way. He had two things in his favour - firstly he had no competition and secondly everyone remained keen to ingratiate themselves upon his wife Louise, who was a senior flight attendant at a major airline.

'Well, we must stick to protocol, hands up for the Hawk. Motion carried. Congratulations, oh and remember me to Lou,' said The Badger nudging and winking his way to discounted flight tickets.

'Yeh, Barbados is nice this time of year.'

'So are Sydney and Melbourne.'

'We love Benidorm,' added Dave 'Whitey' White to laughter and shouts of 'you need to widen your horizons.'

The Badger banged his now empty pint glass on the table and said, 'so now to the main event what. The election of the first team captain.'

'We only have one candidate for this position too, your current skipper Barry Briggs.'

I stood and nodded graciously as my name was read out to a smattering of applause.

'But, in the name of fairness, I need to ask if there are any other candidates in the room.'

I found the suspense excruciating; a bit like at a wedding when the vicar asks the assembled freeloaders whether anyone had any previous with either party. The crowd in the bar-cum-tearoom strained their necks to see whether I would have any challengers. The minutes ticked slowly by and, just as The Badger was about to close his account, the front door opened and in strode ex-skipper Matt Williams.

CHAPTER 2 - THE VILLAGE

I quickly recovered my composure.

'Uh hi Matt, bit late, aren't we?'

'Well, I heard you were 24 hours early mate', he countered, sending the assembled into convulsions.

1-0   to the ex-captain.

'Well yeh, Noodle wanted to play bowls yesterday instead.' I countered.

'Actually it was the bowls club AGM, not a match you numpty,' countered Noodle.

Luckily for me, The Badger interjected and welcomed him to the fray, explaining that they had just asked for challengers to my captaincy and whether his timing was an indication of his willingness to step into the breach.

'Oh no Badger, I have just finished dinner at The Prickly Oyster and thought I would pop in and see how things were going' he explained, prompting me to utter a sigh of relief and equally one of disappointment from the baying crowd.

'Ok, ok so people let's finish this, are there any other candidates?' asked The Badger. The ensuing silence filled me with a warm glow and soon I was starting my fourth season as first team captain of Buntingford Smedley CC.

I rose gallantly, wiping a false tear from my eye for effect, started to thank my fans for their support, walked to the bar and opened my laptop.

'WTF are you doing Baz?' asked Alfie Aikins, the stout first team opening batsman, 'it's a dull-arsed AGM not your office'

'Well, Gilo', as Alfie was called on account of him being a farmer and all farmers are called Giles, 'I have prepared a framework on how I would like the first team to operate, and I think it will benefit all the teams. In fact, I ran it past The Badger in a private meeting, and he is in full agreement.'

'Sod that pal, I need a drink' countered Gilo as he rose from his seat, adding 'me arris hurts from sitting down for the last three hours listening to yous all wittering on about bollocks.'

And with that Gilo rose and this led to everyone else following suit, bringing the meeting to an impromptu conclusion. I sighed, closed my laptop and went back to my seat, narrowly avoiding Gilo's right boot just as The Badger brought proceedings to an official close with a ceremonial thump of his fist on the table and pronounced that the first round was on him, and that he would settle up later.

I probably need to tell you a bit about me and our village of Buntingford Smedley, since they form the basis of my story. I was born in a little hospital in the nearest big town, which you can reach by taking the number 92 bus from the stop in the village's market square. We are too small to have a train station and so the bus has always been a vital transport link to the neighbouring towns and villages. My parents, who were also born here, worked in the Campbell Brewery, and so didn't earn enough money to be able to buy a car, so my first journey in this new world was by bus, as it had been for them.

The village was mentioned in the 11th century Doomsday Book. I have taken the extract, as frankly I don't understand what it says, and any translation would leave me open to ridicule from Noodle, who probably thinks that the Campbells are mentioned.

In the Hundred of Plumbleigh

Buttingfordesmedelei.

St Harold held it before 1066. Then as now it paid geld for 1 hide. Land for 2 ploughs. In demesne 1 plough, 2 villans and 4 bordars with 1 plough. 2 slaves. Meadow for 5 oxen. Woodland for 3 swine.

There is 1 mill rendering 5 sesters of meal. A pasture lies beside the stream. There is a hall, 1 church, poor.

The land is worked. The ploughs go in season. Was worth 12 shillings, now worth 6.

Held now by the king's reeve under the lord.

I later learned that as the Campbells were a Scottish clan from Argyle who would not rise to prominence for another 200 years, I probably needn't have worried about Noodle's opinion. To be honest, I shouldn't in general, but he really is a moustache-twirling horror show and so you constantly needed to be wary in his company. Unlike The Badger, who had fathered two sons, both of whom currently worked at the brewery, Noodle had been unable to produce any offspring. In a way, that was probably a good thing, but it added to his sense of inferiority to his brothers, for there were another three of them scattered about the precinct.

As I was born here, along with my wife, the Stevens brothers, Gilo, Biffa, Gobshite and a few others, I was always interested in the history of our village, its people and their stories. That's why I thought that I would start with the Doomsday Book, although a popular archaeology television programme had come here a few years ago and found some Roman and Anglo Saxon remains. At Briggs Design, my little marketing agency, we had created the materials that had accompanied the exhibition that followed, and Ella and I had featured on TV as a local crew had come to film a small feature for their news programme. She had taken great pride in explaining to them that it was her dad who had made these posters, a statement that caused some Monday morning consternation amongst our design team.

Without the Noodle worry, I did try and translate the Old English and found out that St. Harold was a monk, who had constructed a monastery where the manor house was later built. When William the Conqueror's troops rocked up, he was asked to bugger off and the Normans took his land, which was about 120 acres in today's terms. I am not sure how big that actually is, but Gilo would tell you that this was enough room for a cow to go missing twice in one week. There seemed to be a couple of ploughs to go around, one which the new Norman overseer kept for himself and the other shared liberally about the few villagers that existed. I had thought that the villan that they mentioned was some sort of village baddie, maybe one of Dazzler's ancestors, but it turns out that this was a peasant farmer tied to the land, who toiled all day for little money, so not like Dazzler at all. They were assisted by bordars, who were even lower down the social ladder and not posh school boys abandoned by their wealthy parents. I thought about my kids and how easy their lives were in comparison to those of our ancestors.

Today's Church of St. Harold stands on the same site as the old church mentioned in the Doomsday Book, but I would have imagined that it would have been a wooden hut in those days. We had gone down to the churchyard when we were children and played games amongst the graves. Again, I imagined my tablet-bearing children and their addiction to wi-fi.

So to summarise the village in those days, it had a bit of land, a shed-cum-church, a feudal chief and some old lags with dodgy knees, waiting for the day to end so that they could have a beer in the pub. Not unlike today's cricket club in reality.

I don't suppose much happened in the intervening years, apart from a family called the Cholmondley's rising to power and building a manor house in the 1600s on the site of the derelict monastery. There are rumours of the ghost of an amply proportioned, wine swilling monk haunting the manor to this day. This may account for the second lord's teenage daughter running off with a farmhand from Pillingsbury. The first lord of the manor had married the daughter of the landowning Smythe family and in order to preserve both family's legacies, they joined their names and the Cholmondley-Smythe dynasty was born. The manor is now defunct, having suffered a great fire in the 1800s, with just the bell tower remaining. There are some Cholmondley-Smythe's living in the village now, we went to school with a couple of them, but they don't use their title or anything.

Instead the nearest we have to village nobility is the Campbell family, who rose to power through their brewery as I had previously mentioned. In 1750, Angus Campbell had decided that he had enough of making illicit beer from the wheat that he had threshed for Sir Walter Cholmondley-Smythe, whose son's actions would unintentionally lead to the start of our cricket club, and approached the genial peer with a plan. Together they formed a company and Campbell's Brewery was born, making beer from the local wheat, which was rare in a time when barley was the primary grain used. So together they became rich, well richer in Sir Walter's case, and started to supply the shires with Campbells' Wheat Beer and thus put Buttingford Smedley on the map, where it solidly remains today.

So whilst the Cholmondley-Smythe's have pretty much disappeared from the social scene, due in main to Sir Harold's actions, which I will explain later, the Campbells have risen to great heights. Angus became a knight of the realm and became Sir Angus Campbell, although The Badger is not Sir Colin, whereas the Cholmondley-Smythes that we went to school with are technically Sir Paul and Sir Christopher, one of whom is the nominal Lord of the Manor of Buntingford Smedley. But given the lack of any physical manor, he can't exactly strut about the village asking for obedience and the like.

Jonathan 'Jock' Campbell, the father of The Badger and Noodle, had played a major part in adding other beers and a cider made from local apples to the brewery's production lines and turned it into a national enterprise. The Badger had an older brother, who had been killed when his motorcycle had collided with what had remained of the manor, and so, as second in line The Badger was recalled from the army to be primed as the next managing director. He only had to wait a matter of weeks, as his father decided that he was too old to run the business, stepped up to be the chairman and handed the keys over to his successor. The Badger had appointed his brothers in key roles, including Noodle as finance director, before the latter had decided that he wasn't being paid enough and started to remunerate himself through some extra-curricular activities. I was only a boy, but I remember my parents coming home from work to relate the tales of Jock Campbell marching his errant son out of the brewery, kicking him up the backside and telling him to never grace these gates again. The Badger, who couldn't stand up to his father in public, instead decided to help Noodle by giving him positions in the bowls and cricket clubs instead, which is how we came to be stuck with him.

After me, my brother and sister came, both born in the same hospital as me and also arrived home on the 92 bus. I had started at Buttingford Smedley Primary School by the time my sister, the youngest of my siblings was born, and was already playing football and cricket in the playground with Flash, although he was plain old Greg then and Sam. Alfie, who was later called Gilo, Adam, the future Gobshite although he had potential then too, and The Badger's boys all joined in our lunchtime and weekend games. Our dad's followed their fathers by playing football and cricket at the weekends for the Buntingford Smedley clubs, and so that is what we also did. That is also where I met Jane as she was friends with my brother at school and her dad also played cricket with mine. We all used to play in the nets as kids and stayed as a tight little group as we progressed through to the local senior school and attempts at getting served under-age at The Prickly Oyster.

It came as a major surprise to me when Jane, who I had then known for 11 or 12 years, asked whether I would accompany her, on the same 92 bus, to the cinema at the weekend as there was a film that she really wanted to see. I had assumed that we were all going, the whole gang, but when I turned up at the bus stop in the market square that day, she was standing there alone.

'Where are the rest?' I had asked.

'Where are who?'

'Gilo, Flash, the gang, aren't they coming?'

She had given me one of those looks that would be omnipresent throughout our future lives together.

About three or four years later we were married at the Church of St. Harold, where we had both been christened, and a couple of years later Ben popped out. He broke a long-standing tradition by coming home in our newly bought car, and our blissful coupledom was broken by wailing and nappies. Jane had been working in the Prickly Oyster, and I had travelled daily to the next big town, where there was a design agency who had some nice clients. When Ben, and then Josh and Ella, were born, Jane became a stay-at-home mum, and I decided to start Briggs Design in the village to be able to help more with our growing family. I had never had my own company before, and little did I know that this would mean more work than when I worked for someone else.

But we managed and I continued to play cricket in the summers. I had also played football in the winters, but stopped that, on the advice of my wife, after Ben was born. Jane, of course, was comfortable at the club, having spent pretty much every summer weekend there with her family as well as mine and those of most of our friends. Flash and Sam's parents would come with a large, tartan picnic blanket and hamper that always contained delights out of the financial reach of my parents. They were a lovely couple and would happily share any of their treats with us kids, although Ginger, their Red Setter dog was less than impressed with this. Whilst Farmer Aikens was agriculturally dispatching bowlers across The Wreck, his wife would hand out the freshly made scones that she had made for the mid-innings tea, an event that is steeped in significance and local prestige as you will soon find out. Alfie, Gilo if you remember, and his brothers and equally robust sisters would form a guard around their mother, not to protect her in any way, but to restrict this ample distribution of scones to all and sundry. Jane's mum, Jill, sat chatting with my mother, whilst her dad Mike was demonstrating his unique bowling action to a bemused opposition. I think that her dislike of me started in those early days, especially when I hit her on the head with an ill-directed shot from our little boundary game of cricket. Her hair pins had coming flying out and dress had been splattered with the whipped cream that emanated from the Victoria Sponge cake as the ball finished its dramatic journey.

With this as our childhood, it was no wonder then that we children soon replaced our fathers in the men's teams. Doug had been the captain of the third team, where we all started, but soon we had shown enough ability to play for the seconds and eventually for the first team, where The Badger was the leader. I would like to tell you that I had learned a lot from him and that I could put that to use in my future tenancy. Unfortunately this was not the case, and we played some of the worst cricket in the club's history under his leadership, or lack of it, which was surprising given that he was the managing director of the Campbell Brewery at the same time. There was the time, when we played Kingly Down and a number of his workers were in their side, whilst we had a few of the management team amongst our number. The ensuing match would go down in the annuls of local cricket until it was superseded by the cheese incident that I will tell you about later.

I remember that we won the toss on a scorching day, the summers always seemed hotter when we were younger, and The Badger, who I later learned, had been inspecting the local produce in the Frog and Princess pub before the match, decided that we would bowl first. Normally on a hot day, a sensible captain would choose to bat first, but The Badger was anything but rational. The Kingly Downers, mainly the brewery workers took great delight at hitting our bowlers, chiefly their management, to all parts of the village, taking particular aim at the fleet of company owned cars in the parking lot.

'Got the bastard,' one of them shouted with glee, who I later found out was Gobshite Senior, as he smashed the ball through The Badger's car window. Noodle, who had been in the team that day, decided to avenge this deliberate act of vandalism by confronting Gobshite Senior, who had been a keen amateur boxer in his day, and soon learned that a left-right combination at lightning speed had an immediate impact with his verticality. He dropped to the floor, stunning the management executives on our team and, as The Badger flapped, the proletariat took it upon themselves to further attack the company cars. Twenty minutes later the match was abandoned, the fire brigade was hosing down the blaze and the local constabulary was inviting the workers back to theirs for a chat. The Badger, in all of this time, had simply walked back to the pub and revisited his previous testing, saying that 'he may as well as he couldn't now drive home.' But that incident marked the end of The Badger's captaincy as the club hierarchy decided that he wasn't fit, or generally sober enough to be captain, and that he would be better served on the management committee. So he was promoted to club secretary and Matt Williams, a local solicitor, installed as first team captain, where he remained until my investiture.

I think that this covers pretty much everything, and you should be an expert now in the village and how I came to be re-elected as first team skipper of Buntingford Smedley Cricket Club.

CHAPTER 3 – THE DEFECTION

We had had a couple of long, cold months since the AGM and cricket had not played any major part in my daily routine save the weekend working parties at The Wreck to repair the winter damage caused by the football team and to get the ground ready for the summer.

Most Saturdays, and some Sundays, I tried to rouse my troops into putting their tablets down and coming to help alongside the other families, after all it was their club, as The Badger had put it.

'I can't seem to get the kids interested in helping out,' I said, warming my hands on a mug of instant coffee.

Jane was priming the vacuum cleaner for some vigorous morning action, whilst I continued to lament the lack of help from my family.

'Maybe if you came up and helped, they would too?'

Jane turned on me, and with no toning down of her peculiar ferocity she said, 'I spend my whole bloody week cleaning up after you and the kids and if you think that I am going to then help you to clean the clubhouse then you are a massive....'

I didn't hear the end of her sentence as she had turned on the vacuum cleaner, but I was relieved to have missed whatever adjective that she may have chosen to describe me. I had tried to bribe the kids once with a trip to McDonald's afterwards and it did work, but on that occasion, Josh found a spider relaxing behind an old football sock in the dressing room and had run out, screaming for his life. That put an end to their help.

So, I drove up there unaccompanied, to join other reluctant club members escaping their less than willing families into helping prepare the facilities for the forthcoming season. We were given tasks such as painting the exterior of the pavilion, unclogging the showers from mud and worse, and putting up the training nets, all on the inconsistent promise of a bacon sandwich and a free drink.

The Badger was instrumental in arranging this weekend adventure, but he had disappeared after a couple of weeks, leaving me to organise the work, whilst he swanned off to warmer climes. Most people watch the national cricket team toil on TV or listen to the dulcet tones of the commentators on the radio, but The Badger, Noodle and some of their cronies at the bowling club had joined a tour party to the Caribbean to watch the action in real life, as it were. An ex-professional player led the group, and each paying guest had the opportunity to sit with this faded star whilst wearing lurid group t-shirts and exposing pasty flesh to the powerful foreign sun.

The match was being shown on the office TV, which I had more of an eye on than the proposal I was supposed to be writing and happened to be watching the action when a camera picked up The Badger and Noodle who were dressed as described and sporting a shade of sweaty pink.

'Look at the state of them.' I chuckled at how uncomfortable they looked. I imagined Noodle turning his nose up at anything local and asking for chips with everything, although he would have been happy with the best rum that the local distilleries could produce. I looked out onto a grey car park glistening with rain. I was jealous of course.

To prepare myself for the season, I had put myself through a strict regime of vigorous exercise, including thrice weekly visits to the local gym, where I huffed and puffed my way through various classes and a weekend run. I backed this up with a diet that included reducing my beer intake and increasing my protein, which had created some sort of warm wave of joy, which flooded through my system daily.

'Dopamine,' I read aloud, 'Want to feel more motivated, focused, and unstoppable? Boost your dopamine – it's the neurochemical rocket fuel your brain's been craving'

'Well, you haven't been your usual grumpy self, so something must be working.'

I was pleased that Jane and the kids had noticed this uplifting change in me, but I sensed that she, in particular, was wary that this dopamine high would come crashing down as soon as the season started.

Our veteran opening bowler Gordon 'Blacky' Blackwell, conversely, had taken an opposing route by simultaneously increasing his beer and his pie diet, both of which he swore were part of being British, which was a major part of being Gordon. I was in The Prickly Oyster, the better of the two village pubs, one night with Hawk and had overheard him lamenting the state of the nation with a group of his friends.

"Too many people in the country,' he was saying and, with a tut and a shake of the head, stated that 'they had let too many people in and that they should all be sent home. Except those who played cricket for England. They could stay, of course.'

This sentiment was generally agreed with nods of

heads and murmurs of assent from his audience.

'I wish I had written a note about inclusivity in my manifesto,' I said to an aghast looking Hawk, who we had so nicknamed on account of his surname being Kestrel.

'You'll need more than a note to sort Blacky out.'

'Sad but true mate. Fancy another beer?'

'No thanks mate, it will depress me further.'

I nodded in assent, downed the rest of my pint and, as I was walking to the door said to Blacky 'see you, fit and ready to go at nets tomorrow, Oswald.'

I didn't see the confused look on his face for I was already at the door, but did hear one of his friends say, 'I think he meant Mosley.' Blacky probably took that as a compliment.

The gym at the Sir Angus Campbell School, named after the Campbell ancestor who had set up the local brewery, an irony not lost on many, doubled up as the indoor nets for local cricket teams and the car park was already full as Pillingsbury, our arch rivals, had use of the hall an hour earlier and were just coming to the end of their first training session of this pre-season. But the first person that I bumped into was Blacky.

'Hi Blacky', I said cheerfully, 'how was the pub last night, stay long?

'You know I don't like being called that,' countered the middle-aged medium pacer. 'Call me Gordon or Gord. But not that, alright?'

'What about Oswald?' I asked sardonically and, before he could answer, continued, 'looking forward to the season?'

'Not really. Too much traffic, shit teas, too many people in this country, can't bloody get anywhere now.'

'Good to see that you are as positive as ever,' I said, and was about to walk off when my evening took a turn for the worse as the next person that I encountered was the Pillingsbury captain who was leaving the hall, pulling a large cricket bag.

'Finished already?' I asked, hoping to get an early dig in at my nemesis.

'Evening Bazza,' he said, not rising to the ill-disguised barb, 'good session that, lads have wintered well, Gonzo was sharp today, must be the new vegan diet he's on, all those carrots given him laser eyesight.'

This last comment elicited a snort and a muttered comment from Blacky. 'Bloody vegans, vegetarians, foreign muck, what's wrong with fish and chips?'
For once we took a unified stance in shaking our heads and wishing each other the best for the season, not meaning a single word of it.

I walked into the hall, leaving Blacky to light up one last cigarette before entering the coliseum. The rest of Pillingsbury were just finishing off some slip catching practice and packing up as I plonked my bag down and started to unpack my kit. Slowly, the rest of our members turned up, each in turn dropping their bags, greeting me and starting to perform a set of uniquely personalised warm-up exercises.

There is a peculiarity to these warm-ups, and I use the term loosely, dependent on what role you performed in the team. The bowlers, for example, were unified in going to the bag of practice balls and carefully choosing the one that would be perfect for their own particular need. The selected item had to be the right size and colour, with a perfect seam and, after some tossing from hand to hand, a declaration was made that it was the right one for them. They then limbered up in one of two ways - Blacky and wily, veteran spinner Bill 'Chocks' Tillwell performed a strange windmill motion with their bowling arm and declared themselves ready, whereas the younger guys marked out their run up, bowled a few looseners in the nets, added an extended follow through for effect and walked back to make sure that their phone had captured the moment.

For the lesser educated in cricketing terminology amongst you, the seam is the stitching around the ball which the faster bowlers use to make the ball deviate when landing it on the pitch. It is also used by spin bowlers, who grip the seam to impart maximum spin and cuts to their fingers.

I noted that the batters were less vigorous in their warm-ups and our two openers were getting padded up and practicing shots that they would never dare play out in the middle. Greg 'Flash' Stevens, for example, was dropping down onto one knee and practicing a 'ramp shot', whereby the batter attempts to scoop the ball over the wicketkeeper for four, or maybe even a six, but more likely resulting in a trip to the local hospital's emergency department.

Flash was the older of the two Stevens brothers and could have not been more different than Sam, who was only eighteen months younger. We had all been at primary and senior school together, before both brothers and me went to the local Sixth Form College to gain some A Levels. Sam went off to University, before coming back to work at the Campbell Brewery Company as a research chemist, whilst Flash had decided to forego any further attempts at education and had joined a local insurance brokerage, owned by their cousins, and proceeded to forge a career in selling cheap insurance to wealthy land owners.

'Nailed it mate,' he said to a bemused Dazzler, 'you won't be bowling that one there to me or you'll go for loads pal'.

Dazzler just smiled and made a mental note to bowl one exactly 'there' and see what Flash did with it, fully expecting the batter to take one flat in the face. I say that both batters were practicing shots, but I slightly exaggerated as Gilo was still straining to get his trousers on, as they had mysteriously shrunk over the past six months due to his dietary choices, mainly consisting of a fry-up and beer.

'Come on Gilo, we only have the nets for an hour.' I chivvied.

And after grunting something about having a word with 'me missus' about her misuse of the washing machine, he finally pulled up his zip, decided that the top button was best left open and donned his protective padding.

Both gladiators were now ready and walked into their respective nets, waiting for our bowlers to get to work. I was standing at the back with the other two captains, waiting to note down any exceptional performances or those whose character I thought would be perfect for the brand of cricket that I had stylised in the SADFUC document. I would have my turn to bat later, but for now I had a watching brief.

'This is going to be interesting,' I said to the other two captains, who grunted indifferently.

The first ball of the net session was bowled by the second team's star player, Dave 'Whitey' White, who sprinted in and bowled a full ball to Gilo, who swung his bat in a smooth arc and violently dispatched the ball back over the bowler's head and sent it crashing into the back wall. The onlookers ducked and smiled in unison as Whitey adopted a double tea pot stance in the middle of the wicket, before marching back to his mark whilst adjusting his wrist position as he had seen the pros do on the TV.

'Shot Gilo' cried out several of the guys to the annoyance of Whitey who looked around to find someone to pick on. And that person was Simon 'Winners' Winston.

'Got something to say, then say it to my face,' Whitey shouted, his face getting redder.

'Alright mate, bugger me I only said 'shot Gilo''

'Let's see if you can do any better, your lot always reckon you are better than us.'

'Our lot' said Winners, knowing full well that Whitey was referring to his Jamaican heritage, 'have produced some of the fastest bowlers in the world, and you, my son, are going to find that out quite soon.'

After twenty minutes of concerted efforts by the bowlers and T20 style slogging by the two opening batters, I called a halt to their turn and the next two went into the nets. On his way out, Flash winked at

Dazzler and said, 'see I told you that I can play the ramp shot.'

This was entirely true, as Dazzler had kept to his word, bowled a full ball to Flash, who had dropped his left knee down to the ground and with a deftness of touch, scooped the ball up in the air. However, the expected four or six did not occur quite as he had imagined, for rather than flying over and above an imaginary wicket-keeper, the ball sailed high into the roof of the net and came crashing down onto his lidded head, causing him to topple over and Dazzler to break into what can only be described as an assassin's smile.

If you aren't aware of the various forms of cricket, let me fill you in. There are lots – five days, four days, one day, half a day, no wonder people are confused. But the one I alluded to is T20, or twenty twenty, the half day variant designed to bring a new audience to the game, but in reality exists to bring new cash.

Whilst I am on this scholastic journey, a lid, to which I referred to above, is a protective helmet that is worn by batters of all ages and abilities, apart from anyone over 60, who feel that they have the experience to counter any short bowling and that they never had to wear one before so why should they now.

Our next two batters in the nets were our wicketkeeper Adam 'Gobshite' Cottrell and Flash's calmer brother, Sam. As the nets had mixed bowling, i.e. what we called fast but really was anything but, and spin, the next bowler to Gobshite was our talented young spin bowler, who was waiting patiently, flicking the ball from one hand to the other. He started his slow walk to the crease, performed a dainty jump and delivered a looping off break to Gobshite, who thrust one firm leg straight down the wicket, heaved heavily across the line of the ball and duly missed it completely. The offending object struck him on the pads, prompting the bowler to emit a celebratory roar to indicate he had succeeded in getting Gobshite out, LBW.

As always, I found, this form of dismissal generally causes the most consternation at club level. The basic concept is that the ball pitches in line with the stumps and, if it hits the pads instead, then the batter is out. However, the whims of club level umpires are such that the above is made more complicated than it should be, due to a lack of the umpire's knowledge of the laws and dubious eyesight. An off break is a type of delivery bowled by a spin bowler, whereby the revolutions imparted mean that upon landing the ball deviates left to right, or is that right to left? One of them anyway.

'That's plumb, you're out mate,' and, just to make sure his meaning was fully understood, the bowler raised his right index finger at the stricken batter to indicate the dismissal in the same manner that an umpire would.

'Bollocks pal, missing off stump and pitched outside leg, I have kept wicket to you loads of times mate, I know your line.'

The rest of the debate consisted of each player telling the other that they were shortsighted, that they didn't know what they were talking about, and the next ball would elicit the same result. With that Gobshite didn't face another ball for a full five minutes whilst this mid-net altercation was taking place until Winners, the next bowler to bowl to him, impolitely suggested that they save their discussion for another time.

'Keep Gobshite gobby,' I had written, meaning that I wanted him to wind up the opposing batters in the hope that they played a false shot and succumbed. This was to prove to be very true in the coming months, but not in the way that I had hoped.

In the other net, Sam Stevens was quietly going about his business, hitting the ball cleanly and passing encouragement and advice to the bowlers. Occasionally he would need to step back and ask the bowler to pause because Gobshite had missed the ball completely and fallen into the net, which meant that Sam had to help untangle him as a fisherman would do a flapping bloater.

I was still at the back of the nets watching the action alongside the other two captains. We were sitting on a bench, notebooks in hand, well I was using my laptop, making notes on the players that would make up each team. I had known mine since the AGM and had told the other captains what my selection would look like, aware that Hawk, the second team captain, would be most affected by my choices. As always, the main subject of discussion was Dazzler and how many times he would either be unavailable or simply had not bothered to turn up.

Let me tell you about Darren 'Dazzler' Perkins, an interesting character who belied his increasingly portly frame with a cricketing ability that had once interested the professional game. A short season in the county second team was curtailed by his fondness for a snifter before, during and after the game, which sometimes left him bowling down the Piccadilly Line when in fact he wanted to get to Marble Arch on the Central. Faced with a choice of knuckling down and pursuing a cricket career or cracking another bottle of whisky with the lads, Dazzler chose the latter and soon found that this did not fit with the county's required standards, and he was shown the door. Many subsequent jobs later, ranging from roofing to being a dairy delivery executive, a milkman to you and me, which ended with him stealing the milk float replete with its contents and cash, Dazzler turned up at his parents' house in Lower Buntingford demanding filial sanctuary. He was having a few beers one night at The Prickly Oyster with his old friend Gilo who told him about Buttingford Smedley CC, and so he showed up at The Wreck claiming to be an ex-pro and the answer to all my problems.

Unfortunately, as I soon realised, he was actually the source of many of my problems and so when I told Hawk that Dazzler would be my main bowler again, he was both relieved and concerned.

'Mate, listen. Dazzler is a good bowler, quickest we have got, and he will win us, well you, games. But he is unreliable mate, may turn up, may not and if he does then there is the question of what time and in what state.'

'Unreliable drunkard,' interjected Noodle, the third team captain unhelpfully, 'not the sort we want here at all. Turns up whenever he wants, smelling and looking like he has slept under a hedge, which he probably has. And I can't play bowls with a few members anymore after that ruffian stole and crashed the milk float.'

Any further discussion on his cricketing abilities and general personage was curtailed by a cry from the nets.

'Look out', came the warning as a ball rocketed from the bat of Whitey and careered into the back wall, just north of Noodle's capped head.

'Nearly brained the silly old sod,' laughed Whitey, 'next time.' He accentuated his desire to perform heinous deeds on Noodle by turning his bat into a rifle and firing imaginary bullets in his direction.

'Bloody hooligan,' shouted a now-standing red-faced Noodle to howls of derision.

'Another undesirable sort, lowers the standards of the club, especially when he brings his wife and those blooming kids to the ground. I still haven't forgotten the time that his wife accused me of watering down the vodka,' he continued before adding, 'which she has with orange juice.'

'Anyway, back to the subject,' I said. 'I understand that Dazzler is unreliable, but I can't not pick him. It's a tough enough league this year and we'd be doomed without our best bowler.'

'All well and good,' said Hawk, 'but every Saturday morning we wait and see if he is in any fit state to play, assuming we know where he is that is. If he rocks up great, but if not then I lose a player and I must take someone from Noodle, who in turn has to ask a colt to turn up.'

'And that's a nuisance, because I need to go pick them up, take them home etc, can't even have a pint after the game in case the parents think I have been drinking and driving with their son.' said Noodle, ever the clubman.

'So, we need to come up with a plan on Dazzler, why don't you have a word with him Briggsy, lay down the law. You can see how he reacts to your presentation, try using the brand of cricket stuff, you know how to get the best from him.' suggested Hawk.

'Good idea,' I answered oblivious to the sarcasm, 'I will chat with him now.' So armed with both my laptop and misplaced confidence, I walked over to Dazzler and asked him for a quiet chat.

'Teacher's pet,' shouted Gobshite, followed by a protest of favouritism, both of which I ignored as we walked to a quiet corner of the hall, away from errant cricket balls and curious players. I motioned him to a nearby bench, opened my laptop and pulled up the presentation on my plans for the forthcoming season.

I had rehearsed this speech many times, normally in front of my hallway mirror, ignoring Jane's interjections about me interrupting her viewing of Celebrity Masterchef. So, when the time came to deliver my magnus opus, I imagined talking to myself in the mirror, with each word being crisply delivered and accepted without discussion. Things however did not start as expected.

'Baz, why are you opening your laptop, are we going to watch telly?'

'No Darren, I am going to present what I expect from you. Behaviour, standards, that sort of thing.'

'Cricket's played out on the pitch, not on a screen.'

'Yes, well no, because you watch cricket on a screen too.' I countered, somewhat pedantically but I had been rattled by this start, for it was not what I had practiced in the mirror.

Normally when I commenced my oration, Jane would tell me to shut up as she wanted to see if that bloke from Corrie had put enough eggs in his souffle for it to rise. That I could deal with, but Dazzler has this snarky aggressiveness about him, and I found that a challenge.
I regained a modicum of composure and started my well-rehearsed speech.

'Darren, I want to run our plans for the season past you, what we expect from you and the brand of cricket I want us to play. Let's start with tactics.'

'Is your presentation really called SADFUC?' smiled Dazzler, getting to the nub of the issue. 'Cos if it is then it's quite appropriate innit?'

In my role as founder of my agency, I had stood in front of numerous dubious clients presenting designs ranging from a poster promoting a range of key-cutting tools to an advertising campaign for a local pet grooming and yoga service. I had faced rebuttal many a time and knew that today would be no different.

I smoothed my hair and adopted a leadership sort of posture, remembering a TED Talk that I had watched where someone I had never heard of was pontificating about body language. Armed with this insight, I turned to face Dazzler, thrust my shoulders back to convey a sense of power, leaned in to show that I was engaged and looked at my subject matter firmly in the eye.

Dazzler, who hadn't heard of a TED Talk, let alone watched one, conveyed a sense of fascination bordering on the indifference, which quickly turned to amusement as I, for reasons that I still don't know, stuck out my hand to shake his.

'What you doing Baz? We have met you know.'

Embarrassed, I retracted my hand, wishing I had never seen that talk and how apparently the quickest way to establish rapport and authenticity was to do what I had just done.

'Right Darren,' I started authoritatively, 'I wanted to have this chat, man to man as it were, and discuss the season ahead and specifically your role in the first team. As you know, we had a good year last year and you were the leading wicket taker and, well, we want you to do that again this year. But there are conditions.'

So far so good I thought, as I waited for my opening salvo to sink in. If I was waiting for an engagement from Dazzler though, I was sorely mistaken as my prime asset still had a smirk on his face and was keeping very silent.

'But Darren, what we can't and indeed will not tolerate,' I continued, warming to my task and feeling rather Churchillian, 'is the indiscipline of last year, when we do not know where you are, what state you are in and whether you will even turn up. It's simply not on and, if you want to play for the club, you need to change your attitude. It is firmly up to you.'

With that, I leaned back, satisfied that my words had the desired effect and awaited Dazzler's response. In the background, the nets session had gradually come to a halt as the tension building in our corner had begun to waft its way towards the rest of the group, who in turn had put down their weapons and had started to walk over to where the real action was taking place.

Dazzler, having observed the previous posture that I had adopted, opened his shoulders, leant in, made strong eye contact and offered his hand, which I accepted warmly and rather smugly.

'Well Bazza, thanks for the speech and all I can say is that you will have nothing to worry about this year.'

I felt that warm dopamine-rush sensation throughout my body as I sensed that my preparation had resulted in a speech worthy of note and was indeed going to deliver the desired outcome, vis a vis a reformed Dazzler.

Ever the showman, he turned away from me and, after pausing for effect, addressed the now fully formed crowd.

'You won't need to worry about that Bazza, because this year, I'm going to play for Pillingsbury.'

CHAPTER 4 –
THE FUNDS

I remember the stunned silence. You could hear a pin drop, followed by mutterings of mutiny and discontent from the crowd in the Sir Angus Campbell School gym. The aftershock of Dazzler's treachery had subsequently reverberated around Buntingford Smedley and the surrounding villages, especially Pillingsbury, which was feeling collectively smug at having acquired a new opening bowler of such quality. But it had come at a price, as he had negotiated himself a nice transfer fee and a weekly pay-as-you-play contract that the committee would need to rubber-stamp before he could don the colours, well whites, of his new club.

I don't know if you have ever come across such committees, but they exist up and down the country and they generally turn their collective noses up at such nefarious activities because the finances of any amateur sporting organisation are perilous at best, and Pillingsbury and Buntingford

Smedley are no exceptions.

'The expenditure is still very high, 'lamented the club treasurer. 'Constant upkeep of the ground, fuel for the roller, wages, maintenance of the building, it all mounts up. We can't keep increasing the annual subscriptions or the match fees, but thankfully the bar takings are healthy, although the till roll and the cash don't always add up. And with that she cast an eye at The Badger.

'We also need to replace the far side net as it seems to have eaten by foxes, or some other creature,' I added, keen to ensure that my side had adequate facilities for the Tuesday night training sessions.

'Yes, that too,' said the treasurer, making sure that this was not high on the list of her immediate priorities.

'What do you propose that we do about this lack of cash?' asked The Badger, keen to regain his moral high ground and simultaneously avoid any suggestion that he should put any money into the coffers of the club that he held so dear.

The ensuing silence and inspection of fingernails were interrupted by an eager Tim Kestrel.

"I have a couple of suggestions. We could have a front of shirt sponsor like they do in the football, maybe a local business, and we could also get a side of ex-professional cricketers to come and play our first team alongside a family fun day.'

'Marvellous ideas from the Hawk,' enthused The Badger and, again keen to make sure he was only involved in the glory and not the heavy lifting said, 'you can form and lead the committee in charge of Operation Top-Up.'

Tim Kestrel was a mid-level manager at a global haulage business and as such was used to petty committees and mass levels of bureaucracy. In fact, he revelled in it and so accepted this invitation with a certainty that he could bring clarity and organisation to the fundraising committee.

Even though there was no official process of forming a committee as far as the statute was concerned, The Badger stood up and ceremoniously convened Buntingford Smedley's first ever fundraising committee.

'Well everyone, I think that the Hawk here has proposed a couple of jolly decent ideas and, in my capacity of chair of this wonderful club, I hereby declare the formation of this Operation Top-Up committee' and, without any fear of mixing his metaphors, said 'I wish all that who sail in her the best of fortune and to make the village and club proud.'

Hawk's first task as chair of the event sub-committee of Operation Top-Up was to appoint some foot soldiers who would actually do the work, which entailed delivering sponsorship income and organising both a celebrity match-cum-family fun day.

Not wanting to waste any time, he went straight into action by standing up and making his first appointment.

'Baz,' he said.

'Tim,' I replied.

'Baz,' he repeated

'Still here.'

Silence ensued, before Tim then said, 'I know that you would want to be involved.'

'Right so far,' I thought.

'I was thinking whether you would be best suited to raising sponsorship or organising the event.'

All I really wanted to do was meet some of the stars that would make up the celebrity cricket team and wasn't that fussed about bouncy castles and candy floss. I hoped that Hawk, my friend, would see this and make a sound decision, but my dreams were thwarted when he proposed that I should add the post of organising the family fun day and cricket match to my CV.

Having seized the floor, he continued with quickfire appointments suited to what he perceived to be individual strengths.

'I think that Winners and Bread should run the

sponsorship deal as they are both entrepreneurs and would know how to do these things,' suggested Hawk to be met with approval from The Badger and the club treasurer, the former already impressed with himself for appointing such an astute leader of the event sub-committee.

Simon 'Winners' Winston and Ian 'Bread' Daly were two local lads who had made themselves a small fortune through creating the impossible, that is to say that they invented dustbin bags that actually fitted the bins, and through this had built an empire.

Noodle though was less impressed with giving such fiscal responsibility to two people that he considered 'flighty' and without a 'proper job' between them.

'Why on earth would you give those two such responsibility,' he scoffed. 'They don't even have a job, I mean they sell dustbins or something, at ridiculous prices I may add. Find someone else Hawk.'

'Over-ruled,' countered Hawk with authority, 'unless of course you want to do it Noodle?'

'Nicely done mate,' I thought, and as Noodle, despite spluttering, did not have an adequate response, The Badger brought the meeting to an end and we bought ourselves a pint and went to find a quiet corner, in an empty room, and started to plan the event.

'Ok I need to get in contact with the Wandering Has Beens,' I suggested, 'they are a team of ex-pros who play charity matches etc. They should bring in a crowd.'

'How much will that cost?' asked Hawk, 'I'm concerned that the objective of raising money for the club may be swept away by, um let's see, well that is to say, you wanting to further your cricketing connections.

'Rubbish,' was all that I managed, secretly knowing that he was of course right.

'And also, don't forget the family fun day, bouncy castle, a BBQ, maybe some craft stalls, that sort of thing.'

'Yep, got it' I said, instantly relegating craft and hot dogs stands to second place after the pro-am match.

Muttering that he would need to keep a close eye on me, Hawk picked up his mobile and called Winners to explain the sponsorship plan and how he, and Bread, were the most suited for that task.

This meeting had taken place after the first Tuesday practice that I had decreed as compulsory, especially for anyone wanting to be considered for first team selection. The members had netted indoors at the school gym over the winter months and had moved to outdoor training at The Wreck. Not wishing to start off on the wrong foot, the entire first team squad had trained along with a smattering of second teamers and not a single third team player, who were simply following the lead set by Noodle, their captain, who spent Tuesday playing bowls instead.

Selection for both the first XI's pre-season friendly against Thrustbury and a combined XI versus The Lock and Dungeon public house followed and, after we had formulated the Operation Top-Up committees, we went home with misplaced confidence that this year would be a great year for BSCC.

At breakfast the next morning, I brought my family up to date with the possibility of meeting famous cricketers that they may have seen on the TV. Ben, as you can imagine, was excited and immediately pulled out his sticker book.

'Is he coming Dad?' he asked, pointing to the current Indian captain.

'Uh, no son, probably too far.'

'What about him, I like him'

'No, he's banned son' leading Jane to look up at me from her knitting before our eldest could ask why.

'Those in your book are current players and those coming would have played in the past but may include former an England captain or two.' I explained.

Ben put his sticker book away, somewhat forlorn.

'Are they all old and wrinkly then? Asked Ella, adding 'like granddad.'

'No not that old,' laughed Jane before Josh asked whether then they were 'old like dad?'

I got up from the table, leaving my middle child's question hanging in the air, and helped Jane clear away the breakfast things, before ushering the brood towards my car and onwards to school.

After arriving at the office, I opened my laptop, which soon pinged with an email from Hawk, attached to which was a spreadsheet entitled 'Family Fun Day Project Map.' I downloaded the attachment to my desktop, renamed the file 'Celebrity Match and FFD' and opened my browser to find out the best contact at the Wandering Has Beens.

Winners and Bread had also received an email from him, entitled 'Sponsorship CRM,' attached to which was a spreadsheet containing columns for name, company, value and status so that they could keep Tim updated with the outcomes of their efforts.

'Bloody hell mate, the Hawk could be worse than Bazza, who'd have thought it,' said Winners addressing his partner on opening the attachment.

'Don't sweat it, let's just create a small presentation and email it out to local businesses.'

And with that, Winners and Bread spent the morning temporarily abandoning their successful disposables business and focused on creating a document to win over the hearts, minds and budgets of local businesses.

I, on the other hand, had grand ideas about ex-England international captains gracing The Wreck and teaching me and Ben a thing or two about the great game. So excitedly, I had reached out to the Wandering Has Beens, who said that someone would call me back, and, with less excitement, had asked my PA to contact purveyors of bouncy castles and assorted fun day items.

Saturday and the match versus Thrustbury came and went. We had put out a strong team and enjoyed a resounding win against a much weaker opposition with some of our star players getting much needed boosts of confidence with runs and wickets. Afterwards we drove back to The Wreck for a pint and a debrief. However, Hawk had other ideas on how we should celebrate our win.

'I thought that we would have this weekly meeting to make sure that Operation Top-Up was on track,' he said, unaware that weekly meetings were vital in making sure that the pace of progress was as slow as possible.

'Let's start with our sponsorship supremos. Winners, Bread, how have you got on with your efforts since Tuesday?'

'Well, we have created a little document outlining our offer and have sent it out to local businesses,' replied Bread to expressions of delight from Hawk, who nodded knowingly.

'Yeh we've identified all of the assets that our club has to offer, both on shirt and off, and valued them all,' added Winners, unhelpfully.

'Ahh yes, good, good, yes, good,' stuttered Hawk, 'and what about you Baz?'

'I have contacted the Wandering Has Beens to find out what dates they have open and Bonzo's Bouncers to get their availability too. I have also asked my PA, to speak with her friends in the village and organise a bring and buy sale.'

'Excellent good, yes, it's all coming together then,' concluded Hawk and brought the meeting to an end after ten highly productive minutes.

Whilst Winners and Bread were quite happy with their progress to date and were sure that they could convince local businesses to partner up with their local cricket club, I, on the other hand, was apprehensive and wished that I hadn't agreed to be part of Operation Top-up after all.

I needed to confide in my wife and tap into

her wisdom. As pre-season friendlies are low-key affairs and not many players go back to The Wreck post-match, I arrived home early.

Jane had been preparing tea, sorting out the kids and had just found 15 minutes to put her feet up when I returned scowling. I dumped my cricket bag by the front door, poured myself a drink and slumped down next to Jane, who got up to pour herself a glass of wine in preparation for what was bound to follow.

'I need your help Janey,' I started, deciding that the direct approach would be the best course of action. 'Tim has made me head of this event organisation and frankly I don't know where to start. I took it on as I thought that it would be good, for Ben you know, to meet ex-pros and learn about what it takes to succeed. But Hawk wants tombola, food stalls and a bouncy bloody castle. I've asked my PA to help, but need you too,' I said, adding a belated 'darling' to layer on the need for Jane's assistance.

We have been married for 15 or is it 16 years and had met at primary school, so we have known each other a long time. But even after all these years I struggled to accurately place Jane's looks and the one that she was fixing me with now seemed to be a mixture of pity fused with love, a combination that is uniquely mastered by the female of the species. But I wasn't sure and frankly never will be.

'Baz,' she started, then stopped. Her original response was going to ask how the bloody hell he thought she could fit any more into her week but then decided that she could help by asking her friend, who owned Crafty Mary's in the town, if she could organise some stalls for the family fun day.

'I can ask Mary to arrange something,' she said calmly and if Bonzo comes through with the bouncy castle, then you are set.'

'Yeh, I guess so, I need the Wandering Has Beens to confirm a date and then we are good,' I said and got up to have a shower, feeling that I had made great inroads into the plan, leaving Jane to wonder whether she should just get the bottle of wine instead.

It was Sunday morning and Winners' inbox pinged with an email from the Taj Mahal Indian restaurant. He opened it to see that the sender was a Mr. Mohammed Ibrahim, the proprietor himself who was a big fan of Buntingford Smedley CC and wanted to help in any way that he could. Winners replied to ask when he would be available and, even though the restaurant was closed on a Sunday, the proprietor himself replied to suggest that this lunchtime was perfect.

'Fancy a curry?' Winners messaged Bread, who replied in the affirmative and thus the club's first ever sponsorship meeting was confirmed.

I was strolling across the market square just after noon, taking the family for coffee and cakes at The Sacred Scone when I saw Winners and Bread being let into the closed Taj Mahal. I thought it somewhat odd, but didn't really give it any further consideration apart from maybe they were trying to sell Mohammed Ibrahim some dustbins with matching liners.

'Welcome Mr. Simon and your friend, what is your good name?' enquired the proprietor of Winners.

'Mr. I mean, Ian,' replied Bread, 'just Ian.'

'Well Mr. Ian you too are also most welcome to my humble little restaurant.

And with that, they were offered a seat at a table for four and Mr. Mohammed Ibrahim picked up an ordering pad and came to join them.

'I am afraid that we are closed on a Sunday, a time for my cooks to rest after a busy week. But it gives me time to cook the books and make some other business.'

Winners and Bread, who had both skipped breakfast in anticipation of a Sunday Balti, tried their best to hide their disappointment and thanked the proprietor himself for the alternative which was a Manchester United mug containing sweet chai and a copper dish half-filled with some store-bought Bombay Mix.

'I was fascinated by your proposal,' said Mr. Mohammed Ibrahim, and as a fan of the cricket, as all we Bangladeshi's are, I wanted to see if I can support our local club.'

'That's great Ibrahim, may I call you Ibrahim?' asked Winners.

'Please,' said Mr. Mohammed Ibrahim graciously, even though he preferred to be called Mr. Ibrahim 'continue.'

'Thank you, well as you may know we have a strong local club with three adult teams and a strong children's section featuring both boys and girls. The first team, of which myself and Ian here are members, are in the third tier of the county league with a strong chance of promotion.'

'Inshallah,' intoned Mr. Mohammed Ibrahim and continued, 'yes, I know a few members of the club Barry, Colin and his idiot brother, they come in quite often, generally with their wives and are good payers. Also come in are some other boys, they are more like ruffians and make the hullabaloo. But they drink plenty of beer and we learn to put up with them, they are all nice boys really.'

Having labelled most of the members of the cricket club accurately, Mohammed Ibrahim continued, 'but you see, the problem with the local cricket is like this – no TV and no publicity for my restaurant. You want me to pay you money and in return what do I get?

'Very true,' said Bread, all business like, 'but what we can give you instead was laid out in the document we sent you.'

'Please explain it to me, I would like to hear it from you.'

'Well we have three teams, plus training kits which can give you publicity all over the county, and also you could name the ground – The Taj Mahal Wreck has a good ring to it.'

Mr. Mohammed Ibrahim smiled, he had been in these situations many times before and knew that sponsoring the shirts of the Buntingford Smedley teams was a waste of his money and the Taj Mahal Wreck wasn't doing anybody any favours.

'We local businesses should support the local clubs and societies. By doing so we foster a sense of community and maybe overcome some of the issues we face in today's world,' he remarked stoically.

Winners and Bread sat back thinking Mohammed Ibrahim was a bit of a soft touch and that the deal was done. 'Maybe they should have negotiated a commission with Tim if they were all going to be this easy,' thought Winners

'However,' continued the owner himself, 'I do not think that what you have proposed is worth the

£2,000 you have outlined in your document. So, I have a counter proposal for you to consider, and it is like this. I propose that all three teams have the Taj Mahal Indian restaurant logo printed on their playing shirts, we will of course cover the cost of this and, instead of paying for the privilege, we will give the club dine-in vouchers, conditions apply, to the value of £2,000 for members of the club to enjoy a fabulous culinary experience in the restaurant.'

Winners and Bread were not sure what to make of the offer from the shrewd restaurateur. On the one hand there was no cash on offer, but on the other, the club members could enjoy free curry, although they were sure that The Badger would pocket the majority.

'Thank you, Ibrahim, we will consider it,' said Winners eventually, and stood up to shake the proprietor himself warmly by the hand.

'You are too kind,' he replied, before adding 'I had already mentioned this to Mr. Colin, and he said it was a good deal and that I was to ask you to bring me the shirts so I can give them to my cousin Saeed for the printing purposes.'

'W-w-w-what,' spluttered Winners and Bread in unison, 'why did you tell us about community spirit etc then if the deal had already been done?'

'I like the TV programme The Dragon's Den, and

when I am watching I am imagining that I am the big shot businessman who is making the deals with youngsters inventing all sorts of this thing and that thing. I thought I would be one of these dragons peoples even though I know that the deal is finished already.' he explained to the exasperated duo.

'Maybe you can bring the shirts tomorrow and I will have them returned by my cousin Saeed on Thursday?' And with that he beamed a wide smile, thrust out his hand and congratulated the duo on their business skills.

Winners and Bread staggered out into the bright sunshine that was bathing the market square of Buntingford Smedley and bumped straight into our family returning from tea and sugary delights at The Scone.

'Hello Uncle Winners, Uncle Bread,' said Ben to the still overawed duo. 'Did you have a nice lunch? We go there sometimes,' he continued blind to the lack of eastern sustenance offered on a Sunday, 'I like the butter chicken, but Josh thinks it's too hot, Dad has the...'

Before he could recite the entire family's culinary preferences, Jane held up her hand and simply said 'thank you Ben,' to which her eldest ended his attempts to ingratiate himself with the two cricketers he admired the most.

'What was going on in there, I thought they were

closed on a Sunday, selling Ibrahim bins and bags were you?' I asked suspiciously.

'Went in to try and get them to sponsor the shirts, but it turns out that The Badger has got there first,' explained Bread, who then went on to explain the underhand dealings that had transpired.

'We now need to try and round up everyone's shirts by tomorrow and give them to Ibrahim to get them printed.'

Jane shook her head, mimicking the actions of anyone in charge of the domestic laundry, and rolled her eyes in the knowledge that my cricket shirt now needed to be prioritised over the children's school uniforms. I, on the other hand, was excited by the news that my first team and, de facto my club, would be one of the few to have a sponsor on their shirts. We would look especially smart when we played the Wandering Has Beens in the family fun day.

'I'll get my guys to send them theirs, if you call Hawk and Noodle to do theirs too.'

Thankful for my assistance, the intrepid sponsorship executives, set about calling Hawk, who was amiable and would organise the second team's shirts and then they called Noodle, the third team skipper.

'YOU'VE done what?' he shouted down the phone.

'Well technically we didn't do anything Noodle, your brother....' retorted Winners, realising that he may not have been the best person to break the news.

'You leave my brother out of this, you two morons were tasked with bringing reputable, LOCAL, businesses to the club and instead you bring us this,' he snarled, continuing, 'and if you think that I will be wearing the logo of THOSE people on my shirt, well, well, you are very much mistaken.'

As the conversation was taking place on the speaker, Bread had heard everything and grabbed the phone from his friend.

'Noodle, what this reputable, local cricket club does not need is people like you, stuck in the 1970s wearing your Union Jack singlet and Dr. Martens, spewing hate and making life difficult for everyone. Your brother did the deal, as Winners said, so go and vent on him. In the meantime, collect the shirts from your team and leave them at The Wreck tomorrow by 6pm.'

'Now look here,' spluttered an irate Noodle, not used to being spoken to in that fashion.

Winners looked at his friend with renewed admiration, which rose to new heights when Bread closed with a 'there's a good boy,' and cut the call.

'Haha good work mate, and, thanks,' said Winners.

'Well, he gets away with that all of the time and someone needed to say something,' responded Bread, and with that the fearless duo boldly went to find some food.

The first and second team captains spent the next hour of their Sunday afternoon calling their teammates and arranging for their shirts to be collected. As the vast majority were either in the wash or still in their bag, which may or may not be in their immediate possession, it was generally agreed that each member would drop their shirt off at The Wreck during Monday and that Winners and Bread would then take them to Mohammed Ibrahim, where they hoped that their industry would be rewarded with a free curry, authorised by the proprietor himself.

The third team members had received no such call from their captain, who instead had called his brother, The Badger, who was enjoying a post lunch port at Ye Olde Millstone, the quieter pub in the village, with his wife, the Mayor and the lady Mayor.

'Hi, all ok?' he asked with trepidation that the answer may well be ruinous of his hitherto pleasant afternoon. And he was right. Initially, he just listened to his brother, motioning to his lunch party that he would be a couple of minutes, but as the call continued, his face started to change from its ruddy post-port rouge to chardonnay white then to Burgundy red leading to concerned looks from his wife. The confident 'I'll be a couple of minutes' was replaced by an apologetic wave of his free hand and a silent mouthing of the word 'Paul' to signify that he would need to step away momentarily. He went outside to give himself both some fresh air and the opportunity to say what he really thought and, if you were say a family of four with two kids under ten, then let's say that you may have to uneducate them over a few choice words and phrases.

'Just get it done,' finished The Badger and, still fuming, he strode back into the bar, downed his glass of port and demanded another, at speed.

Therefore, when Winners and Bread arrived to meet Tim 'Hawk' Kestrel in the bar-cum-tearoom of The Wreck on Monday evening, they were handed three black sacks, each labelled with the name of the relevant team and, after sideways glances, they hauled the sacks into their car, drove to see Mr. Mohammed Ibrahim himself and hung around long enough to be asked whether they would like to stay for dinner.

When I heard of the dressing down that Noodle had received, I was of course pleased, for he was an obnoxious so and so and frankly the less I saw of him the better. But the Campbell family were Buntingford Smedley royalty and Noodle knew everyone that there was to know. No one actually liked him, but they needed to stay on The Badger's good side, and so they tolerated him. And Noodle always took advantage of this.

CHAPTER 5 - THE SEASON

It been a fraught few months for me as I continued the organisation of the celebrity match and family fun day alongside trying to select a team capable of competing in the league. Dazzler's defection to Pillingsbury had hit everyone at the club hard, except Noodle who, still in a foul mood after the learning of the new club sponsor, had celebrated the ousting of an undesirable by writing a letter in The Buttingford & Pillingsbury Times.

'Dear Sirs,' it started, before going on to list several reasons why local cricket clubs should be careful as to who they let join. For example, he wrote,

'Undesirables have recently been let into the country and, as time has gone by, they have infiltrated various parts of this green and pleasant land hitherto unaffected by such issues. As such, the dynamics of the village have changed, and it won't be long before families who have lived here for generations are forced to leave. The cricket club that I love so dear has been affected in recent times with such undesirables, but thankfully one of them has had the good grace to leave and join Pillingsbury instead. Good riddance to him.'

The 'ButtPill', as the local newspaper is affectionally known, then printed a series of replies from residents who questioned whether Noodle had looked in the mirror recently as families who had lived in the village for a long time ran the risk of over-familiarity. He had also considered writing to object to the club's sponsorship deal but had decided that his brother's wrath would be too much to bear. Furthermore, he quite liked a weekend Balti.

All of this however was a sideshow as I struggled to come to terms with the loss of my star bowler. When I had got home that evening from the Sir Angus Tootle School, as Jane would later recount to her friends, I had gone straight upstairs, crashed about hurling kit and clothing akimbo, woken the children up who had enquired whether Daddy was drunk again, and then collapsed on the floor weeping tears of frustration.

'What's wrong Dad?' a concerned Ben had asked, having led his goggle-eyed siblings from their beds.

'It's over son, it's over, I tried, we all tried, but it's over.'

I hadn't obviously meant to distress them, but they had been genuinely concerned. Were their parents going to split up, what would happen to them, would they be sent a foster home and be made to wear Sergio Tacchini tracksuits? Before this nylon nightmare theme had fully matured, Jane had come upstairs and ushered them back to their beds telling them, in a comforting fashion that, 'no Mummy and Daddy were not getting divorced, just that Daddy must have had a cricket club related disaster and that she would deal with it.'

'What's the matter Baz?' she had asked.

I had been sitting quietly on the floor, using the breathing techniques that I had read about in the pet grooming and yoga advert that we had developed. I had discovered that accessing one's subconscious through controlled breathing was less than easy when you had a river of snot running down your nasal passage. I had taken a deep and disgusting sniff and looked up at my perplexed wife.

'He's gone,' I had said dramatically, 'left us, gone.'

'Who?" Jane had asked, kneeling next to me concerned that someone from the club had met their maker and that I was genuinely distressed.

'Darren Perkins,'

'What happened?'

I had paused for dramatic effect. 'He's joined Pillingsbury.'

As I write this, I remembered the next sequence of events all too clearly. She had stood up, hands on hips and had surveyed the room with a slow, determined movement of her head. Her eyes had come to rest on one of my cricket bats that was reposing peacefully in the corner. She had taken a couple of deliberate steps towards it and picked it up like an axe.

I shouldn't have said what I said next, but it was too late, it had already slipped out.

'You don't hold it like that,' I had sniffed.

She had fixed me with a withering stare, exhaled loudly, launched the bat at me and went back to pour herself a glass of Chardonnay and console herself in the misery of The Apprentice, leaving me to soothe my bat in the knowledge that my evening had just diminished further.

Over the ensuing days and weeks, I tried, along with The Badger to persuade Dazzler to return to Buttingford Smedley, using liquid incentives to lubricate his thinking. However, even though the errant speedster was happy to accept beers and whiskies he was steadfast in his desire to play for Pillingsbury, leaving us searching for a suitable replacement.

Two candidates came to mind, both from the second team, and these now formed the entire agenda of a high-powered summit that had been arranged at the Taj Mahal Indian restaurant. In addition to me, the delegates were The Badger, Hawk and Noodle.

'Evening all,' said Noodle as he threw his hat and coat to the nearest waiter with a haughty flick of the wrist. He took his seat at the table and looked around at the illustrations of Indian village scenes depicting villagers drawing water from a well and tigers chasing farmers from their fields.

Shaking his head he said, 'I don't know how these people still live like that,' and clicked his fingers to summon a beer from the waiter.

Even though they are brothers and share the same DNA, The Badger is a lot more reasoned, explaining why he was the chair of the cricket and bowls club, of the parish council and various charitable organisations. I don't know what he thinks of Noodle, but his normal reaction, unless pushed, is to ignore him and continue as if nothing has happened.

'Well gentlemen, we are assembled here to find a solution to the unfortunate situation that Darren has left us in.'

'Don't know why we are bothering,' interjected Noodle.

'Yes well, the whole village read your views. I am surprised that you didn't moan about the Taj Mahal sponsoring the kit. Although I see that you are happy to eat here.' I pointed out.

Noodle was about to answer when The Badger interjected that bickering wouldn't help and that they had tried their best, but the stubborn speedster was intent on playing for Pillingsbury.

'So now Briggsy and Hawk must decide who gets promoted and who stays in the seconds.'

With that he leaned back, folded his arms and observed his two lieutenants in action.

'Right mate,' 'I think we will be better off taking Bread and you keeping Whitey.'

'But you will be taking our best bowler, and we are light on bowling as it is.' countered Hawky, desperate to keep Bread and lose Whitey, who despite being his best player was also his biggest pain in the arse.

My response was interrupted by the waiter bringing drinks, some complimentary poppadoms and chutneys and asking if they were ready to order.

'Give us 15 minutes, if you would, my good man,' The Badger asked and regally waved his hand, bidding me to continue.

'I hear you, but we don't need more batting, we need an opening bowler and so we need Bread.' I too was desperate to avoid having to put up with Whitey's grandstanding behaviour every given

Saturday.

And so, the great debate rumbled on, perpetually interrupted by the increasingly frustrated waiter, with neither party willing to capitulate. Eventually there was a winner, i.e. the waiter who eventually got his order, but we two captains were no nearer agreeing who would be promoted. It was left to The Badger, as chairman and recently self-ordained head of selection, to rule.

Well chaps, I have listened to both sides and decree that Bread will be given his chance this weekend and that Whitey will be considered as soon as possible.'

And with that the food arrived, piping hot and spicy to match the mood of Tim 'Hawk'Kestrel.

Things had worked out quite well in the two pre-season friendlies that we, resplendent in clean sponsored shirts, had played. I had mentioned that we had beaten Thrustbury CC previously and our next fixture was against Clackington Ford CC. Batting first, we managed to rack up a stonking 250 for the loss of 5 wickets against a team a league lower than us. Flash had scored a jaunty hundred and was ably supported by his brother Sam who stroked the ball to all parts of The Wreck. A mid-summer crowd would have cheered these shots with vigour, however in the April pre-season, the crowd consisted of Mohd. Ibrahim the proprietor himself, his son Kamal, Doug and his dog Dave.

I was a happy little soldier when I put my key in the lock of 42 Kingston Road, Buttingford, dumping my bag by the front door and striding manfully into the living room ready to regale my family with tales of our superlative performance. I had been expecting to see Jane reclining on the sofa with a glass of Chardonnay watching some vapid programme on the TV but instead found her engaged in deep conversation with Louise Kestrel, wife of Tim, popular amongst the members of Buttingford Smedley CC mainly due to her friendly nature and job as an air stewardess at a major international airline. She was also good friends with Jane and I, we all had attended primary and secondary school together and she often came around on a Saturday to lament their lost Saturdays together.

'Alright Bazza darling, did you win today?' asked Louise.

Retrospectively, the answer should have been a simple, 'Hey Lou, how are you? Yes, we won thanks.'

However, I was on a high after our win and still had endorphins pumping their way through my bloodstream.

'Hey Lou Lou, yep big win, lads played well today. Winners took a five-for, Blacky and Chocks two each and...'

I would have continued giving the two totally disinterested ladies a player-by-player summary had Jane not interrupted me.

'Baz, we don't really care love. Just don't leave all your cricket shit by the front door'

I shook my head in a 'you don't understand' kind of way and went to attend to my kit bag as instructed. After taking it upstairs waiting for it to be emptied by the domestic fairies, I grabbed a beer from the fridge and went back to the living room, with my cricket bat and a cloth.

'Did you know that Carol Dexter had run off with that bloke from Tesco?' Jane was asking Louise as I entered.
I mean, I didn't really care either way and apparently neither did Lou, as she and my wife turned to stare at me as I sat down.

'Does Tim do this?' she asked, as I rubbed my bat with warm water, 'after every match, this saddo comes in here, wipes his bat and adjusts his handles.'

'Rubbers' I said pedantically.

'Rubbers then, so to confirm - your Saturday evening consists of wiping down your bat and playing with rubbers?' she confirmed, trying to keep a straight face. Louise, on the other hand, could not and burst into peals of wine-induced laughter.

'Not that I know of Janey, but he does lay his kit out on the bed before a game and ticks it all off on a list'

This caused both girls to convulse into further laughter and me to comment on Hawk's strange habits. After cleaning the red ball marks from my bat and adjusting my handle rubbers, I kissed my bat and took it upstairs to bed.

The week dragged on at Briggs Design Ltd and I could not wait until Saturday morning, when I would lead my team, in their freshly sponsored shirts, out against Bishop's Tackle CC for the first game of the new league season. Friday night was sleepless as I fretted over whether Blacky was over the hill, should Winners go up a place in the batting order, had Gilo heeded my advice on Friday night lock-ins, if I had organised the pick-up time properly and could I put my new shots into action. I did eventually fall asleep, but not before I further irritated Jane after a poorly aimed cover drive, the most elegant of cricket shots, hit her firmly on the thigh.

All this fretting had left me rather jaded on Saturday morning, but I rose with a high sense of anticipation at this first morning of the new season, a special day in any cricketer's calendar. My voice-activated speaker had informed me that the weather was clement and that I and my troops should go out and perform to the best of our abilities. Well, perhaps not the second part but nonetheless I skipped down the stairs like a young colt and greeted my breakfasting family with glee.

'Morning gang,' I beamed, 'cricket starts today. It's going to be a great season; you guys will enjoy it down the club this year.'

This presumption was ill-judged as usual and was met with a collective silence as my children deemed YouTube and sugary cereals as more deserving of their attention.

'You may get a shot at the third team this year son.' I tried, unsuccessfully hoping that Ben would strike up a conversation.

'Josh, what game are you taking round to the Kestrels?
Jane had all this time been leaning back on the counter watching me engage with my children and, when she felt that they had been tortured enough, jumped in and asked them to get ready.

Having wolfed down my breakfast of champions, I

waved them off for their day with the Kestrel kids and walked upstairs to repack my already packed kit bag. I emptied everything out onto the bed and opened my phone, navigated to the list on my note app and checked that I had everything.

All freshly branded clothing was unfolded and refolded, my two bats were checked and the rubbers adjusted, boots were brushed and all other and totally necessary items like sunglasses, zinc cream, wristbands, headbands, stretching bands and gels were packed. A quick shower was followed by the unveiling of my new Buttingford Smedley tracksuit and polo shirts.

Over the winter, The Badger had followed the England cricket team around the Caribbean and been impressed with their attire, and the military man in him had risen to the fore

'Jolly smart they looked, we should get some training kit made and make sure that everyone buys some,' he had suggested to a concerned club treasurer.

So, having tapped up an old friend with some experience in these matters, he proceeded to have made and delivered boxes of cricket shirts, caps, tracksuits and polo shirts. Every member of the squad, especially those in the first and second teams, were encouraged to buy these and wear them with pride on match days.

I started to clamber into my new kit and was somewhat surprised to find that the advertised sizes did not quite match the actuals. My tracksuit top was supposed to have been a large, but appeared instead to have been made for a previously large person who had drunk some of Alice, of Wonderland fame's, potion and had shrunk. To make matters worse, the sleeves were too long, rendering me unable to zip it up, which was probably for the best.

I hoped that the tracksuit bottoms and polo shirt would be a better fit. The trousers were true to form, leaving the purple top as the last remaining article to reveal itself. I pulled it over my head and smiled as it fitted perfectly. I rolled up the sleeves on my tracksuit top, bent down to pick up my bag and was dismayed as the sleeves of my polo shirt detached themselves from its body.

So, wearing an overly tight tracksuit with oversized sleeves and a polo shirt-cum-tank top, I set forth to meet the team as arranged at The Sacred Scone on Bridge Street. As today's match was away at the picturesque village of Bishop's Tackle, which apparently got its name from a 13th century man of the cloth who used some ungodly ways in which to cajole his parishioners into divine submission, I had ordained that The Sacred Scone was a better meeting point than either of the pubs for the obvious reason.

'Gilo man you stink,' observed Gobshite.

'Just left the Oyster, hell of a lock in.'

'Did you sleep there all night? I asked, wondering whether I should mention my non-lock in rule.

"Yeh, but I went home about 9am, quick nap, got changed into this nice new training get up and now I have just finished one of the Scone's famous fry ups.' With that he belched and rubbed his stomach in satisfaction.

'Jesus Gilo,' complained Flash as the output from his opening batter reached him.

I inspected the remaining troops to make sure that they were decked out in the correct attire. I was pleasantly surprised for a smart bunch they were too, even though the clothing didn't always fit the wearer.

'Ere Bread, did you make these?' asked Gilo.

'If we did mate, they would have fitted,' he replied and high fived his business partner, Winners.

As I had said, Bread and Winners were award-winning entrepreneurs who sold their products across the coun
try, making these two young inventors millionaires at a relatively young age, a fact not unnoticed by Blacky, whose frequent request for a beer was always accompanied by references to their financial status.

After a quick head count, we set off for the 30-minute drive to the village of Bishop's Tackle. As the various cars snaked their way along the country roads, I was quiet and pensive, focusing on my tactics for the day, ignoring Gilo and Gobshite's animated discussion as to who was going to get the most runs this year.

It may have been animated, but its intellectual levels were not going to test anyone at Mensa.
'You keep up that lifestyle Gilo you will definitely have the runs, just not the cricket type,' Gobshite had said, prompted Gilo to lean away from him and emit a loud, eggy fart.

'JEHAYSUS,' shouted and anguished Gobshite, trying to push the button down to let some air in. Gilo just sat there, chuckling to himself with his arms around his ample waist.

'Baz, open the window man, I'm choking here.'

I realised that the child locks had been on and soon Gobshite was hanging his head out of the window, gulping in large volumes of fresh air, whilst our tormentor looked smugly on.

Whilst this maturity was taking place, I was mentally rehearsing my SADFUC document and reinforcing what I wanted to achieve, the brand of cricket I wanted us to play and the behaviour that I expected of them. A summary of these thoughts would form the basis of my pre-match huddle and speech. By the time I had reached the end of my imaginary rallying call, we had reached the gates of the Bishop's Tackle ground, and the season was officially on.

The home team were there and had already changed into their cricket whites.

'I bet that they don't have training gear," I remarked to Sam.

'Not like ours anyway,' he replied sardonically

We walked into the away changing room, dumped our bags on the floor and, after some 'howdos' to the club officials parked on benches outside, as is customary, we walked out to the middle of the ground.

I enjoy inspecting the square before the match gets under way, but if you are unfamiliar with this cricketing tradition, then let me enlighten you. The basic principle is to look at the strip, the cut piece of grass measuring 20 metres in length and around 3 metres in width, upon which the match takes place. Batters walk alongside it looking for uneven bits of grass or cracks which might cause them undue concern, and pain, if the ball behaves haphazardly after hitting one of these areas. If you refer to the previous description of the importance of the box, you will get my drift. They then walk to either end, adopt their batting stance and play imaginary shots, ones they are unlikely to play in combat. After a nod of satisfaction, they wander back to the pavilion. Bowlers on the other hand, look at these anomalies with glee and vow to pitch the ball in these areas on a regular basis to inflict maximum pain on the batters. Both parties will also rub their hands on the grass to check the moisture and make an unfounded, yet profound, declaration as to its geological make up and expected behaviour. Opinions are dressed up and delivered as facts, and the older you are, the more gravitas you hold in this matter.

Having finished this inspection, I put down some small training cones on the side of the pitch and beckoned the team over for some fielding drills, causing the Bishop's Tackle team to stop their own warmup of a few stretches and a read of the newspaper to observe this spectacle.

'Come on chaps, let's get warm', I shouted and started jogging between the first few cones, followed by the keener ones wanting to show the right signs, whereas the rest of the team showed a bit more restraint. Gilo to be fair was in the first camp, however Blacky, Chocks Tillwell and Gobshite were less than willing.

'Bloody waste of time', moaned Blacky, 'win the bloody toss, bat first, knock 'em over and piss off home. You don't need all this malarkey. I work all day on my farm, last thing I need is this nonsense ruining my Saturday.

'Worried you might blow a gasket before the match Blacky?' ventured Gobshite.

'Call me that again and I'll gasket you', he grumped, returning to a familiar theme. Gobshite grinned, reminded himself to call him that on a regular basis and trotted off to join his team. Adam Cottrell, called Gobshite for his runaway mouth and caustic humour was your typical wicket-keeper. If he had played rugby, he would have been the annoying scum half that winds up the big opposition forwards and then waits for his own lummoxes to step in and protect him. Whilst he was born in Buntingford Smedley, his family had come from Kingly Down, about five miles away, and so it would take a few generations before the Cottrell clan would be accepted as locals. Unwittingly, Gobshite had taken this as a challenge and proceeded to impregnate various village maidens at an early age and so there were two, maybe three, possibly four mini-Gobshites for him to painstakingly avoid. This avoidance tactic did not work well when it came to both irate fathers of the said maidens or indeed the authorities, who continually chased him to pay for the products of his haste. So Gobshite spent his days working as a labourer, his evenings drinking in The Prickly Oyster and weekends avoiding any paternal duties.

The Bishop's Tacklers had been watching our performance with amusement, vowing never to include that in their pre-match routine of strolling and reading. The most hazardous part was catching practice, whereby I hit the ball as high into the air as possible and called out someone's name, who in turn had to run in and catch the rapidly descending object. Whilst the first few names succeeded, causing the opposition some concern, the remaining catches all fell to the ground and, in the case of Chocks, he fell to the ground as the ball missed his outstretched hands and hit him squarely on his toe.

The resulting squeals and language of such complexity caused the BT chair to rise from his slumber and administer a stern rebuke to the nearest offender, which wasn't Chocks, who was being hauled off the pitch and placed rather unceremoniously in a deck chair, waiting for someone to bring him ice from the bar.

Practice continued, somewhat half-heartedly after this, until I was called to partake in the pre-match toss of the coin to determine who would bat or bowl first.

So, on that early spring afternoon, with the sun poking suspiciously through the white fluffy clouds, I accompanied the Bishop's Tackle skipper to the middle. Even though we had already taken part in the pre-match routine of the pitch inspection, I bent down, with my ripped polo shirt-cum-tank top allowing extra flexibility, and rubbed the grass once more, inwardly deciding it was a 'bit moist.' Chris Dingle, the Bishop's Tackle skipper, produced a shiny 50p coin and, after demonstrating its authenticity, flicked it skywards.

You may know this already so forgive me, but the middle is a cricketing term used for something that is not actually in the middle. It is a term used for the square, which is not always a square but is the grassy bit on which the game takes place and where the stumps are located. Also called the strip.

'Tails,' I called as my eyes followed the spinning disc until it landed on the square with her majesty facing upwards and giving me a disapproving look.

'We'll have a bowl,' pronounced a relieved Chris Dingle, who had come to the same conclusion as I regard the moisture in the strip.

For the non-geological and non-cricketers in the audience, a 'bit moist' means that it is expected to favour the bowling side. The ball will hit the strip, grip and deviate, causing the bemused batsman all sorts of palpitations.

Again, a lot of this comes from years of watching cricket on the TV and listening to commentators talk about the effect the weather conditions have on the ball. The reality at our level is negligible.

As we walked off, we performed a silent dance that was a signal for our watching team members. I performed a solemn batting motion whereas a more jubilant Chris Dingle flicked his right wrist, with the first two fingers pronounced, indicating that BT was to bowl first.

'Well you buggered that up skip,' Flash greeted me whilst putting on his pads and other protective paraphernalia.

'Pitch is a quagmire, it could do anything,' he continued positively, overdoing my more sombre moist prognosis.

I wasn't really paying much attention to him as I was concerned with the state of Chocks' toe, which was wrapped in ice, but upon revelation I saw that it had turned a fine shade of violet.

'It's broken Barry' claimed the veteran spinner-cum-medic, 'I'm out for the season I think.' And with that he gingerly rose and picked up his kit bag, which Sam had kindly packed for him.

'Where are you going?' I asked, not unreasonably.

'Hospital, Barry, I am going to get an X-Ray' replied Chocks, equally reasonably. And with that he was hobbling to Doug's car and the local A&E department.

'Bloody lightweight, he'd be still here if he could catch,' added Gobshite, continuing the season of reason.

My thoughts were interrupted by the pavilion bell, that signalled that it was time for the season to get under way. The Bishop's Tackle team started to walk out onto the pitch in dribs and drabs, followed by home umpire Stan Clarke, Blacky who was acting as an additional umpire and lastly by Gilo Aikens and Flash Stevens, our two opening batters.

To continue my education for those who don't follow the game, it is important to note that at this level of cricket, members of the batting side act as umpires as generally there aren't enough people willing to give up a Saturday afternoon to perform such tasks. Sometimes a local ex-bank manager, like Stan Clarke, volunteers, but the batting team has to still provide an umpire to stand at square leg and fiddle about for 10 overs before being replaced.

The tall, ginger BT opening bowler was standing at the end of his run up at the Pavilion End, tossing the brand new, shiny red leather ball from hand to hand. Flash and Gilo had fist-bumped in their batting gloves and the latter had taken up residence at the non-striker's end whilst Flash assumed the responsibility of taking the first ball. He nodded a brief 'howdo' to the BT wicketkeeper and accompanying slip fielders, a lot of whom he already knew, and placed his bat onto the ground. My nerves were on edge.

'Two please ump' he called, meaning that the 75-year-old, bespectacled Stan Clarke had to guide Flash's bat from 22 yards away to an exact position between the leg and middle stumps.

Tradition dictates that the batsman then scratches at the surface like a hen looking for feed, taps his bat in recognition that the correct spot has been identified and surveys the field like an army general. Some of the more educated batsman will count the number of fielders, not to see if the opposition is cheating, but to see where the gaps in the field were, with the idea of hitting the ball into these gaps and save on any unnecessary running.

I had taken my seat on a large bench, next to the scorer, when umpire Stan looked around the field.

'Let's play gentlemen,' he shouted, and the bowler began his run-up for the first ball of the new league season.

CHAPTER 6 - BISHOP'S TACKLE (AWAY)

'Agghhhhhhhhhhhh'

I had only just made myself comfortable when I heard the entire Bishop's Tackle team cry out in unison. Those of us who were already watching the action stayed transfixed, whilst those who had been buried in their newspaper hastily dropped it and jerked their head upwards.

The ball had left the bowler's hand at around 60 mph, hit the pitch somewhere near Flash's bat and, having heard that the pitch was a bit moist, veered sharply inwards and hit the unsuspecting batter square on his left pad.

The bowler accompanied that monstrous cry by turning towards the umpire, dropping to one knee and raising his arms high above his head, leading to every member of the BT side providing him with vocal support. Flash had retreated from the stumps in a vain attempt to cloak the appeal with doubt. Unfortunately though for him, Stan Clarke was awake, and he slowly raised his right index finger to signify that he was out, first ball of the match and of the season.

The BT crowd on the sidelines cheered at wonderous this start to their season, whilst we groaned as one.

Momentary shock on the batter's face was replaced by anger, followed by some violent bat swishing and colourful language as he started the lonely walk back to the pavilion. The bowler, on the other hand, was understandably cock-a-hoop and, arms flapping like a demented albatross, ran towards his teammates and proceeded to high five them all, if albatross do such a thing.

It was like Ella had played one of her practical jokes and glued me to the seat, for as much as I tried, I couldn't get up. The shock was too much. The best that I could muster was to look to my left to make sure that the next batter was ready. However, all I saw was chaos.

Generally, whilst the ground scratching is going on by the opening pair, the third batter gets ready, hoping not to be called into action for a few overs. They, along with the rest of the team, settle down on the provided benches or chairs, with newspapers and other reading materials, and prepare to watch their opening batters accumulate runs - bat big and long was the popular terminology. However, when the opposition strike with the first ball of the match, the outcome is like throwing a hungry fox into a chicken coop.

'Oh arse, where's my box?' flapped Sam, the next man in.

'You're wearing it,' retorted Gobshite, staring at Sam's crotch and shuffling uncomfortably.

'Oh yeh, thanks mate where's my lid, I brought it out with me.'

'It's by your bat,' I said, shaking my head at the confusion and wondering whether Sam was in any state to face the next ball.

Whilst this lesson in non-preparation continued to unfold, the fielding side was looking on keenly, and not without some amusement, waiting to see when the next batter would come to the crease. Eventually, gear in place, Sam Stevens walked out onto the Bishop's Tackle field ready to face the music.

Flash reached the pavilion, silently walked past the murmurs of 'bad luck' and 'did it do much' and plonked himself down onto a bench.

'Tossing, toss, toss,' he said.

'Exactly,' I replied, unsure as to what to say.

'Bugger me backwards with a rotten sausage, that moved a mile.'

Gobshite uttered a low groan at this last statement, causing Flash and I to look over at him momentarily.

'Unlucky that mate,' I consoled and went back to my bench, a worried man.

Sam, in the meantime, had reached the middle and was engaged in a mid-pitch conference with Gilo.

'Did it do much?' Sam asked, expecting Gilo to have paid any attention to the one and only ball he had seen to date.

'Dunno mate, wasn't really looking,' came the unhelpful answer.

Understanding that this would be the full extent of his knowledge, Sam went through the previously described routine of asking for a guard, scratching like a rabid hen and counting the fielders, who incidentally were of the same number and in the same position as five minutes ago.

The now emboldened bowler started his run up and released another ball, with which Sam decided that he was not going to engage. Instead he performed an extravagant leave shot, like the ones that he had seen on the TV and walked to away reflect on whether the photographer from the ButtPill had captured it.

I ought to explain that a leave is where the batter decides to move their bat out of the way of the ball in the most extravagant manner possible. It is considered one of the best shots in cricket, odd as it isn't actually a shot at all, but is in fact a leave.

The rest of the over continued in pretty much the same fashion, ball pitching somewhere in the same postcode as Sam, who declined the invitation and walked away to contemplate life.

Flash had now removed his pads, gloves and any other protective gear and had decided to go for a stroll around the boundary edge with Gobshite. I was pondering on what this unlikely couple would have to talk about when the umpire called 'over,' with a level of self-importance he considered appropriate to his standing.

They say that cricket takes ages to play and a lot of this is due to the in-between overs break. It is of course necessary as the umpire must walk from one end to the other, the batters have to meet in the middle and punch gloves before discussing what they would do that evening, and the bowling side must be manoeuvred into position. All this takes time and skill and is certainly not to be rushed.

Even though the first over hadn't gone exactly to the plan that I had laid out before the match, I felt a bit more relaxed having seen how calmly Sam had played the remaining five balls. However, this feeling of tranquillity evaporated when I saw that the bowler at the Wrinkly Bishop Pub end was someone who had a fearsome reputation in the local leagues.

Graham 'Singles' Singleton was somewhat of a local sporting legend having played football at a semi-professional level, representing Tackle Athletic FC in the FA Cup, played golf off single figures and bowled left arm slow. At 65 years of age, he strolled in off five or six paces and delivered the ball at roughly 20 mph, slow enough to cause it to change temperature mid-flight, but covered with vast amounts of mystery and disguise intended to fool the batter. To add to this intrigue, he was a competitor and used every verbal and physical trick available to bamboozle his foe into playing a rash shot and giving up his wicket. You can see why I was concerned and to emphasise this, I got up and started to pace about fretfully.

After setting his field, he marked up his 'run' and twirled his arm around, signifying his readiness for the task ahead. Gilo, whilst all this had been going on, had performed the required hen scratching routine and was currently nonchalantly leaning in his bat, waiting for Singles to bowl. Eventually all interested parties were ready, umpire Stan Clarke called 'play' and Singles ambled in, released a flat delivery causing Gilo to lurch forwards and block the ball to about 2 inches away.

'No,' shouted Gilo, loudly and somewhat unnecessarily given the ball was currently located next to his big toe. The reason for this call was to inform Sam that a quick single was not required at this juncture, thank you.

Now, communication between the two batters is a vital part of the success of any team, but like every other amateur set up, we don't practice it at all, but after today's match I may include it in my manifesto. Calls are meant to be loud and decisive and intended to convey a clear and precise intention of what is expected by both interested parties.

The best analogy that I can give you is a set of traffic lights. So imagine that a call of 'Yes' is indicated by the green light and is therefore a signal to run, similarly when 'No' is called, then it is a red light, and you are to stay put, and finally a call of 'Wait' is the amber equivalent. However consider then the traffic light is faulty, and you get a true indication of what happens in the middle. Any of the three calls can be suddenly changed and this where the trouble usually starts. The problem child is 'Amber Wait', which is usually followed by either 'Yes' or 'No,' and if the former then sometimes the number of intended runs is shouted - 'Wait, Yes One', is a common call, clearly laying out the agenda for the next minute or so. However, some calls are not as clear as they could be, for example 'Wait, Yes, No,' is a recipe for disaster and is usually followed by stern looks between the batters. A call of 'Two' followed by a late change of heart, leading to a 'No, One' results in either or both of the batters stranded mid-pitch leading to disaster and the requisite expletives. Now that I have made that clear, you can see that Gilo's loud and steadfast 'No' was clarity in itself and was greeted with a murmur of approval from his teammates.

Singles, with his next delivery, bowled what is commonly known as a grenade, a ball that is thrown higher in the air, making the batter believe that it is eminently hittable. Gilo was of this opinion and his eyes lit up at the sight of the ball arcing through the blue BT sky awaiting the thunderous impact of his cricket bat. As soon as the grenade landed it was off again, flying through the air sailing over Singles' head, bouncing once and clattering into the sight screens at the end of the ground.

'Shot Gilo,' I shouted, 'keep going mate.'

Applause broke out from the rest of our contingent, which had recently been bolstered by Doug and his dog, Dave, who had both declared themselves thirsty and in need of refreshment.

I have played enough cricket at this level to know that the next ball was going to be crucial. Bowlers like Singles are dangerous and as he marched back to his mark muttering to himself, I started to get a sense of dread. This type of wily old codger (WOC) is considered the most dangerous at this level for they possess what is called nouse, which is local terminology for cricketing and psychological intellect. WOCS believe that they have inroads into the minds of the batters and use cunning to tempt them into misdemeanours. In Singles' case, he believed that Gilo could not resist hitting the next ball hard and high and so if he bowled another grenade, then the batter would be tempted. And he was right.

As grenade number two was whirring its way towards Gilo, he wound up to execute another boundary scoring shot. As the ball pitched, he swung his bat with a violent downward motion and connected beautifully with the incoming object. But WOCs have another trick, namely disguise, and whilst this delivery may have looked the same as the previous one, i.e shiny, red, twirly and grenadey, this time there was a distinct lack of pace, which when you are already bowling slowly is some achievement. Gilo had not considered Singles' application of cunning, and the ball did not sail merrily into the car park but flew high into the azure sky.

'Mine' shouted one of the BT fielders who was running towards the ball, arms stretched out like The Mummy of film fame. I leapt up, mouth open, hands on my head as the fielder reached the required position and was impatiently awaiting the ball to finish its acceptance of the laws of gravity and land safety in his hands. Fortunately for Gilo, act three failed to deliver on its promise and the ball hit the fielder flush on his chest, bounced up and landed harmlessly on the ground, alongside the embarrassed fielder.

'Yes,' instructed Gilo to a startled Sam, who looked up see his 120kg, sweaty, bearded partner careering towards him with his bat dragging on the ground behind him. History indicates that there were two options available to Sam at this point - the first was to accept the call as given and run towards the end recently vacated by oncoming Gilo, thus completing the run and adding one more to the team's total. The second was to ignore the call completely and firmly place one's bat, feet and any other convenient bodily parts in one's crease and effectively sacrifice your partner, for the ball would be thrown to this aforementioned recently vacated end, the bails removed, and batter deemed out.

Sam sensibly opted for the former and set off to the far end, whilst his red-faced partner wheezed past him. The fielding side in the meantime had located the ball, picked it up and thrown it to the end that Gilo was heading towards. The ball clattered into the stumps, resulting in another exclamation of 'Agghhhhhhhh' from the fielders, causing me to drop to my haunches and shake my head in frustration.

Septuagenarian umpires, as you may realise are not the swiftest of creatures, unless retreating from their round at the bar, and consequently umpire Stan Clarke was in no fit position to see whether Gilo had made his ground or not. In fact, he was on all fours, having been flattened by the incoming batter and was scrabbling around on the ground looking for his glasses.

'Not out, not out,' he squealed after regaining some sort of composure, difficult for a seated, temporarily blind retired bank manager.

He was hauled up by an irate Singles, who often wondered why he still bothered playing and an amused Gilo, who dusted him down whilst simultaneously hitching up his trousers and congratulating him on his fine umpiring skills.

On the sidelines, we were not sure whether to laugh at the misfortune of the BT players or applaud Gilo's luck. So, we did a bit of both and sat back down awaiting the next instalment of this enthralling display.

Gilo, buoyed by this early stroke of fortune, went on his merry way, combining agricultural thrashes into the undergrowth with stoic defence and resolute calls of 'No,' which increased in their frequency as he became more tired. Sam's considered innings soon ended, and this unfortunately started a total collapse of our much-vaunted batting line-up.

Bishop's Tackle skipper, Chris Dingle knew that the moisture in the pitch had to be maximised early and so he kept Singles on at one end and brought himself on to bowl at the other. Singles and Dingles were both WOCs who bowled 'dibbly dobbly' which is a somewhat derogatory term for slow, easily hittable bowling. However, when you combine WOCs, DDs and a moist pitch you get results, and soon the two bowlers had decimated our team. Batter after batter strode to the crease to join Gilo, who greeted each one of us with the same advice.

'He's doing a bit skip,' he said when I had made my way to the middle, 'so knock it for one and leave it to me.' This basically means that the bowler is a WOC bowling DDs and the ball is behaving rather unpredictably. 'If you could just nudge it into a gap, we can run a single and I can continue trying to hit the ball into the next field,' he said confidently.

I nodded in acceptance and did as I was told for the

first few balls. I watched carefully as Singles and Dingles, sounding and looking like a jaded 1970s pop duet, went through their repertoire and tried to tempt me into a false shot. But then, the spell of the WOC was cast and the batter, in this case me, fell under its influence and believed that he was more than capable of hitting this DD out of the ground. I was soon to find that I was wrong as I missed the ball completely and heard the rattle of the stumps behind me. My dismissal continued a procession of failure, with just a brief respite as Winners proceeded to follow instructions and build a partnership with Gilo.

I say brief as there was a flaw with Gilo's advice. And that was Gilo, or more precisely his fitness. What the rotund farmer had failed to consider was that Winners was the last of the three younger, and therefore fitter lads in the team, and that the previous two had run plenty of quick singles and consequently knackered Gilo out. When Winners came to the middle, Gilo had given him the same advice but had decided that he was not going to follow it himself and adopted a technique called 'hogging.'

This is an annoying habit where a batter hogs the bowling for the first five balls of an over and then on the final ball, he would nudge it somewhere and shout 'Come One.' This meant that the batters crossed over and, at the start of the next over the same one would be on strike and able to repeat the process. Understandably, Winners was getting tired of this and decided he would do something about it and, on the final ball of the over, when Gilo nudged and called as previously, Winners turned and embedded himself deep in his crease, unwilling to run. He had expected Gilo to stop and return to his crease, after all he would not have gone very far in that short period of time. In reality, Gilo had taken the laws of $E=MC^2$ literally and gained some serious momentum, and turning was a non-starter. His impetus carried him halfway down the pitch and then, on hearing the jubilation of the BT side as they ran him out, all the way back to the pavilion.

I held my head in my hands, Gilo had been our chance of getting a decent score, but with his dismissal our score stood at a dismal 90-7 with just the lesser batters to come.

If you don't know how a cricket score is displayed, then read on. It is always symbolised as a mathematical equation to add gravitas to its status. In this case, 90 runs, points if you must, have been scored and 7 out of the available 10 wickets have been lost. A wicket is an out. So 7 batters are out, and the fielding side must get another 3, meaning they must removal a total of 10 even though a side is made up of 11 members. Hope that is clear. Oh, and in Australia, the score is displayed the other way around, they say 5-90. Who knows why.

'Bugger,' said Gilo, 'I was having fun out there. Bloody Winners, I'll give him a piece of my mind.'
I was wondering which piece Gilo could spare, when he continued 'but there again he's loaded so if I make him feel guilty then, well, free beers for me like.'
Whilst he was congratulating himself both on the runs that he had scored and his cunning, the BT side were punctuating his thoughts with regular cries of 'Agghhhhhhhh' followed by cheers, signifying another successful appeal to umpire Clarke's scant knowledge of the laws of the game. Soon, and before Gilo had removed his pads, the final wicket fell, and a jubilant Bishop's Tackle team led our two despondent batters, plus Flash, acting as the additional umpire, and a dishevelled Stan Clarke off the field to muted applause from our team.

We were all out for a paltry 120, in our first match of the new season, and I trudged back to the changing room to consider my motivational speech for our bowling effort.

Whilst the action had been unfolding on the pitch, a team of volunteers made up of relatives of the BT hierarchy, had been busy in the pavilion assembling various sweet and savoury treats that form the traditional mid-innings tea. This part of the day is considered an integral part of the match day experience, and the reputation of a club can be made or indeed lost by the quality of this mid-innings nosh-up. We would have our own trials and tribulations in this department in the coming week, but more on that later.

I will quickly let you know how traditional economics of a cricket club works. The members pay both an annual subscription as well a match fee, a portion of the latter goes towards paying for their half of the tea costs. Whilst certain financial fiddles have been known to take place, tea financing is considered sacrosanct, and opposition captains pay whatever sum is generally requested. Rogue clubs have been known to charge the price of a sourdough tuna sandwich whilst delivering a curly edged fish paste version, but on whole the tea remains an extremely ethical economic endeavour.

It didn't seem to matter how things go on the pitch, teams tend to perk up a bit when faced with a mountain of free sandwiches, French Fancies and spongey sausage rolls. Batters are particularly happy at this stage as their work is generally done for the day and they can pile their plates high with their picnic pleasures knowing that their afternoon was largely to be spent standing and chatting merrily to their wicketkeeper.

Gilo, I noticed, in keeping with above, had ladened his paper plate with enough ham sandwiches, sausage rolls and crisps to keep his doctor on stand-by and seemed to be making a beeline for me. He plonked himself down whilst I was in the midst of writing down my half-time speech.

'Budge up Skip,' ventured the bearded pork stasher, 'what you writing? Love letter to Jane is it?'

I was deep in thought and either didn't hear what Gilo had said or had ignored it, just as I was paying the Jammy Dodger on my plate little attention. Gilo however, buoyed by his runs had spotted this and, with his empathetic aerial extended to the full, he swiped the biscuit off my plate with a 'I'll have that then, seeing as you aren't eating it' and got up to regale himself with more tea.

The younger members of our bowling attack had not eaten that much as they wanted to be ready for their bowling efforts and keep themselves in full fitness for the post-match beers back at The Wreck and then at The Prickly Oyster, followed by a Taj Mahal special. Blacky however was tucking into all and sundry, making sure that he was getting his money's worth. Two or three times I saw the veteran trundler returning to the trough to pile another mountain of carbohydrates onto his sagging plate. Washed down with cups of tea and enveloped in the tobacco of yet another cigarette, he declared it to be of first-class order.

I thanked tea volunteers and led the team into the changing room for another pep talk.

'Right lads let's get into them from the off' I said, 'you are all well aware that we didn't get enough runs and are a bowler down, but at least we know what the pitch is doing and how they bowled on it,' I added tactically.

Gobshite turned to Gordon 'Blacky' Blackwell and said 'both ends for you then Blacky, oh I mean Gordon' referring to the fact that Bishop's Tackle had bowled with WOCs at each end.

'I'm not bloody superman,' said the WOC in question, 'one of these younger fellas need to step up.'

'He's right' I said begrudgingly looking at Winners, and Bread, 'if Blacky here is to bowl his ten overs without a break then you fellas need to give him support from the other end.'

'I told you before, don't call me that,' me grumped.

'Team man, as always,' said Winners.

Nods of agreement and a bout of excited high fiving

followed as we rose as one and walked out onto the BT pitch to take our place in history.

I decided to open the bowling with Ian 'Bread' Daly at the Wrinkly Bishop Pub end and the lanky medium pacer marked out his run and proceeded to bowl a few looseners to the nearest fielder in the hope that this would stop his shoulder dislocating when bowling in earnest.

I stood in the middle with my sunglasses and zinc cream in place, marshalling the troops into their correct positions. The two BT openers were also ready and umpire Stan Clarke, refreshed by Mrs. Dingle's legendary jam scones and a sneaky half of best bitter, called upon the game to recommence at its leisure.

I was convinced that I had the field set correctly when Bread came bounding in like a gangly young giraffe and hurled the ball in the general direction of the batter, who hit it serenely to the boundary for a four, to the joy of his seated teammates who also encouraged him to 'have a look son, plenty of time.'

'Unlucky that Bread' came the cries of support from his teammates, who also added cricketing wisdoms such as 'keep it up there lad, make him drive.' I found this last statement rather odd, given that the batter had just hit a ball of full length (i.e keep it up there lad) for four and we were encouraging their bowler to bowl it there again in the vain hope that the batter, whilst attempting the same shot, would inexplicably hit it straight to someone and be out. Well, they knew from experience I guess, as this is what we had done in our innings.

Bread is a clever chap. As I had mentioned before, he and Winners had become millionaires by inventing bins with bags that fitted and so he wasn't going to be one to just follow the crowd.

'I think he likes to drive skip,' he suggested, based on one ball's worth of data. 'So I am going to try a short one, see how he likes that.'

I could have tried to argue and say something like 'well one ball's not enough,' or 'let's not try too many things too early,' but bowlers are stubborn buggers and will do what they want anyway. I walked away and hoped that Bread was right, which he wasn't.

For he did indeed bowl a ball much shorter and straighter than the previous one and watched in bemusement as it sailed high over the trees and into the garden of Mr. and Mrs. Ted Pritchard, purveyors of the finest cheeses in the county.

The ball took a couple of violent leaps off their

manicured lawn and careered undeterred through the window of their cheese shed, shattered glass flying with gay abandonment and came to a peaceful end in a coagulating vat of Stilton.

CHAPTER 7 - THE BATTLE OF STILTON GORGE

Time stopped that day on the cricket fields of Bishop's Tackle as we all turned in horror to see the ball smash through the shed and splodge into the Pritchard's prized Stilton.

The sound of shattering glass and cried from the field had prompted the resting Ma and Pa Pritchard to hastily abandon their afternoon's nap and come scurrying out to their garden in order to assess the damage.

Cheese had, for probably the first time in cricket's glorious history, stopped play.

Stunned into action, we ran towards the Pritchard's increasingly pungent garden, followed closely by the rest of the Bishop's Tackle team, some of whom had stood on the benches to get a better view of the ball's final act. The offending batter however had dropped to his knees in the middle of the pitch and was holding his head in his hands, wailing softly to himself.

Flash, ever the combatant, had put in a solid sprint to reach the fence before anyone else and was surveying the destruction with astonishment and not a modicum of joy.

'Did you bring the crackers?' he asked Gobshite, who had just reached the scene himself and was watching in some wonder as the Pritchards, having inspected the damage to both shed and cheese, had started to march towards the fence with the full intention of confronting the culprit.

The Battle of Stilton Gorge was about the begin and the crowd of onlookers was growing in preparation of some afternoon's entertainment.

'Now listen here you chaps,' spluttered Pa P, 'there'll be hell to pay let me tell you, hundreds of quids worth of cheese ruined.' He then added somewhat unnecessarily in my view 'don't think that you're going to be getting your ball back in a hurry.'

Chris Dingle and I, plus some of the BT committee, who had been snoozing peacefully in the pavilion arrived and proceeded to take charge of the situation.

'Alright Ted?' asked the Dingle, hoping to open proceedings on the right note.

'No, I'm bloody not,' countered an irate Pa P.

'You look cheesed off Ted,' volunteered Gilo, eliciting both muffled guffaws from the assembled and a withering glare from Ted for his troubles.

'Look at this mess,' Pa P said whilst pointing to his shed, which was now emitting an intoxicating smell of ripening Stilton, 'who's going to pay for my lost earnings eh?'

'That's right Ted, you tell them, 'chipped in a defiant Mrs. P, who was standing holding her hip in place with one hand and, worryingly, holding a long metal rod with the other, I later found out that this rod, a cheese iron to the uninitiated, was to remove a core from the cheese for testing its texture and smell. I can tell you without any doubt that she didn't need to test the latter.

'Sorry Ted, accident you see, well he just gave it a proper whack and well anyway I am sure we can sort it out after the match,' said the Dingle, who wasn't exactly sure how they would, but his primary concern at this stage was to finish a game that his side looked like winning quite easily.

On the other hand I was not so keen, given our losing position, and sensed an opportunity to slow proceedings down and maybe even get an abandonment. I stepped up to the fence authoritatively and introduced myself to Ted Pritchard with a tactical question designed to create said delay.

'Hi there, Ted, I believe, I'm Barry Briggs captain of Buntingford Smedley and I was just wondering what effect a leather cricket ball has on Stilton, or any other cheese really?
The crowd of cricketers, officials, onlookers, well onlooker and dog, turned their heads, and in some cases their bodies to face Ted Pritchard, awaiting his response. They sensed that a ripe bout of cheese-related, verbal jousting was about to ensue, and they were not going to miss it for the world. So, with bated breath, they awaited the county's number one, celebrated cheese maker to reply with fact, science and vitriol.

What the crowd saw was Ted P looking at me, trying to ascertain whether I was in full control of my faculties whilst I was trying not to let the smirk on my face grow into a full-blown grin. This stand-off continued for about 15 seconds, until Ted broke it.

'Are you taking the piss?' at which I felt my face redden somewhat and heard the onlookers chuckle.

'The effect that a leather ball has on Stilton, or any other blooming cheese as you asked, is to ruin the bloody thing and set me back hundreds of pounds.

That is what leather does to Stilton, any other stupid questions?'
I had no come back to that put down.

I was only asking,' I mumbled, thrust my hands into my trouser pockets and lowered my head to avoid his and everyone else's gaze.

Tensions between those on the garden side and us on the field of play were escalating, but an unexpected ceasefire arrived in the form of the person who had created this carnage in the first place.

The offending BT batter had appeared quietly on the scene, having gathered some of his composure and faced the irate cheese mongers.

'Sorry dad,' mumbled Paul Pritchard, to our astonishment, 'I'll clear it up after the match, won't be long at this rate, can we have our ball back so we can continue please?'

Realising who the destroyer was, a smiling Mrs. P lowered her rod wielding arm and walked slowly to the fence and gave her son a big hug, which was followed by a firm handshake from Pa P, his father.

'Don't worry son accidents happen,' he said.

Ma P the turned and came face to face with me.

'Here you go lad,' she said somewhat maternally, 'as you were so concerned about the effect that the ball would have, you can come and get it out and then carry on with your little game.' With that she gave me the metal rod and opened the small gate to allow me into their garden.

'Go on Bazza, get the ball back then,' the crowd shouted, viewing me as some sort of gallant prince who was riding to rescue the distressed damsel (cricket ball) and return her to her rightful castle (the match). Raising myself to my full height I took the proffered rod and walked along the cobbled path towards the stricken cheese shed, accompanied by a full complement of Pritchards.

'Sorry about all the kerfuffle skipper,' Paul said apologetically, 'I have asked them to move that shed loads of times, but apparently the sun shines at exactly the right time for the cheese.'

I glanced at Paul, imagined where Mr. and Mrs. P thought the sun truly shone, and concluded I'd know exactly who to call in a power cut.

'That's right, sun in the west, ripens Stilton the

best,' rhymed Pa P. I made a mental note to fact check that later.

Keeping this thought in mind, I walked to the shed, briefly surveying the broken window and entered the realm of the destroyed Stilton to be met by an almighty whiff of suffering.

The ball had landed just to the left of centre, dispersing the outer rind across the shed, with bits attached to the roof and various cheese-related implements, and had drilled itself a hole to a depth of around 30 centimetres, from where it looked back up at me and assorted Pritchards.

'Was nearly ready, was that one,' growled Ted, who in turn looked at a sheepish Paul, causing his mother to exude maternal platitudes.

Well Ted, leather wasn't a flavour that we had ever considered before, but we may do now. What d'you think?' she asked her non-committal husband.

'Right then skipper, use this here iron to get your ball out and try not to cause too much more damage,' he had said instead.

It should come as no surprise to you that I had never even seen a Stilton in the wild before. Jane buys what little of it we have at home from the supermarket, where it had already been carefully portioned, wrapped and over-priced. Facing this wounded specimen, I didn't really know how it would behave when attacked, but I was about to find out.

I took a large breath of cheese-infused air, coughed, and looked out of the window to see that the crowd had also come into the garden, encircled the shed and were waiting for the outcome of this delicate operation. I exhaled and looked down at the ball nestled at the bottom of the vat and carefully positioned the bottom of the iron alongside it, hoping to lever it out of its comfort zone and roll it to the side. The rod pierced the surface of the Stilton next to the ball and emitted a sort of squelch, causing Ma P to utter a 'careful now son' and me to pause briefly before pushing slightly further. A small fissure appeared where the iron had pierced the area of the cheese that was just about ripe, causing bits of it to crumble away, prompting Pa. P to place both hands on the side of the vat and peer in like a new father encountering his first born, which was ironic given the circumstances that had caused this event in the first place.

The tension in the room was enhanced by the build- up of the mid-spring heat and the heady whiff of the Stilton which was increasing as I pushed the iron further into it, but I was a man used to pressure and took another breath, pushed the iron against the ball and performed a violent flick to dislodge it from the grasp of the cheese.

A large object flew across the room and landed with a thump against the window, eliciting a gasp from the assembled masses who had followed its aeronautical path with interest. Like a golfer hoping that his ball had not landed in a bunker, I peered expectantly into the vat and saw that the ball was still nestled in the cheese but had rolled into a newly formed large Stilton divot.

Laughter erupted from the crowd when they realised that I had catapulted a piece of cheese across the shed and left the ball intact, much to the annoyance of Ma and Pa Pritchard who had followed its flight across the room and had synchronised their head shaking with its landing.

'Never could hit the ball properly,' Winners shouted to accompanying chortles amidst encouragement for me to have another go.

'I'll give you ten to one that it doesn't come out this time either,' said Blacky sensing an opportunity to make some money by becoming an impromptu bookmaker on the unravelling cheese stakes.

'I'll have a fiver to say it does,' said Bread.

'Me too.' said Gobshite, and with that Gordon 'Blacky' Blackwell, dramatically removed his white floppy cricket hat and started collecting sums of cash from all and sundry. After about two minutes of this activity, during which I had stepped outside and placed my own bet, the crowd turned back to the action and waited for starter's orders.

'Right, have another go son,' advised Ma P, 'go careful now, we need some cheese left at the end.'

I looked quizzically into the vat and, upon seeing the ball sitting up expectantly, devoid of any surrounding debris, I decided that I had done the hard work and all that it now needed was a deft flick of my wrist and the ball would fly out. So not for the first time, with misplaced confidence, I placed one end of the iron next to the ball and the other end against the rim of the vat, careful not to dislodge any more Stilton. Happy that my passing knowledge of the laws of physics were accurate, I bashed the top of the iron and propelled the ball upwards, where it flew straight up in the air, not unlike Flash's attempt at the ramp shots in the pre-season nets and was claimed by the outstretched hand of Paul Pritchard.

'Agghhhhhhhh' he shouted, to cries of 'that's out' from the crowd, which had grown as news of this cricket-cheese mishap had spread to the neighbouring houses, whose inhabitants had come to inspect the goings-on and place bets on my attempts at securing the balls' freedom.

'Good catch Paul,' shouted one of the BT players, 'you must be the first player in history to have caught himself out.'

A hushed silence descended on the crowd as the significance of this attempt at humour sunk in. By the laws of the game, the ball hadn't touched the ground and as Paul had caught it, was he technically out?

Only one man could answer this conundrum and that was umpire Stan Clarke, and the crowd turned as one towards where the arbiter of such incidents stood. Well, where he once had stood, for Stan had taken his opportunity to sneak off to the pavilion and was in the throws of his second pint of bitter when the cry of 'Agghhhhhhhh' came from the field of play. He jumped up, spilling his drink over the carpet and ran outside to see why the game had restarted, without its appointed officials, only to see things exactly as they had been twenty minutes previously.

'There he is,' shouted one of the BT players, 'Stan come here quick, need you to make a decision, this lot reckon Paul's out, caught Paul.'

I had made my way outside by this time, relieved

to breathe non-cheese polluted air, to make sure that Stan applied the laws of the game correctly, after all we would benefit from the removal of Paul Pritchard from the action.

A confused Stan ambled over, wondering whether that second pint to add to the half he had drunk during tea had been entirely necessary, and was greeted by a crescendo of voices.

'He's out Stan, ball never touched the ground' I said.

'Rubbish, the vat was on the ground so technically the ball did touch the ground'

'No way, the cheese held the ball up'
'But the cheese was in the vat, so he must be out'

This high-browed and rather technical debate was quelled by Stan.

'Quiet, quiet, gentlemen please, I need to think' he shouted, asserting his authority.

'Oi, and lady,' reminded Ma P.

'Sorry Ma P, well I have considered the facts of the matter and my judgement is that the ball has cleared the boundary rope without touching the ground and so I am giving a six,' and with that he turned to the pavilion and raised both of his arms, indicating the prescribed score, and waited for the scorer to acknowledge him, only to realise that he was in fact standing next to him.

'Ahem, Stan, I'm here, next to you.'

'Ahh yes, so you are,' said Stan turning to face the confused scorer and raising both arms above his head again to indicate the same six as before.

With that, we started the slow walk back to the middle to continue a match that needed some creative captaincy from me to give us any chance of victory.

'Well done Bazza, good work that skipper' came the chorus of congratulations, 'never thought you would get that ball out.'

'Yeh, he's never got any of us out.'

'The only thing he gets out of is buying a round,' it continued.

It was Sam who brought us all back to the harshness of reality.

Hold on lads, where's Blacky he owes us money.'

In the excitement of the appeal, we had forgotten about the bet and Blacky, who hadn't, was hoping that we would continue to do so.

'Cough up then Blacky,' said Gobshite, the first to acknowledge that the portly bowler-cum-bookie needed to hand over their winnings. 'Ten to one you said so that's 55 quid you owe me,' he continued.

The crowd, which during this whole escapade had behaved as one, did not disappoint now and turned in unison to face the accused, who was getting increasingly red faced and flustered.

'Hold on, hold on now chaps,' he countered, 'I said two to one it wouldn't come out and it didn't did it, it flew up in the air and the batter here caught it and so technically it wasn't out, like he wasn't,' he said somewhat vaguely.

'Give it a rest,' said Winners moving towards his teammate, 'bet's a bet mate and you need to cough up, and quickly.'
The crowd, including those who had not taken up Blacky's ill-advised offer, nodded, took a collective step forward and murmured in agreement.

'Well, well I don't have that sort of cash on me lads, come on its just a bit of a laugh, here I will give you your stake money back and we can say that's that, eh?'

I wasn't sure what I wanted to do, one side of me sensed a rare opportunity to put this antagonistic beast to bed, and the other wanted to find an amicable solution that kept our best bowler in the team. I didn't get to make that decision in the end as Winners stepped in.

'Give us our winnings or we will....'

The rest of the threat was drowned out by Ma P's leaf blower which proceeded to blow the remnants of the stilton over the fence, ushering the crowd back towards the pavilion.

'We haven't forgotten either,' shouted a member of the BT team as he ran past. Blacky, on the other hand, was wishing that everyone would forget but knew, deep down, that they wouldn't and that he needed to come up with some sort of plan to raise the required extra £900.

I was deep in conference with Chris Dingle and Stan Clarke, the subject of which was the recently recovered cricket ball, which apart from smelling of cheese, had changed colour to a dark plum.

'Can't use this now Stan,' said the Dingle, 'the ball

has changed, it looks like a sunburnt Edam, what do you think Barry?' he asked.

Even though I sensed that the change in the ball's condition could result in an uplift in my team's fortune, I had to agree, and we decided that a replacement ball would be used. After much toing and froing, a replacement was found and umpire Stan indicated that play was to resume.

It had now been some 40 minutes since the ball had been bowled and I had to chivvy my players, still bitter at Blacky's bet evasion tactics, to focus on the match, but that was easier said than done.

'You need to come up with the cash Blacky' said Gilo, 'or I'll get my thresher out on you.'

The potential recipient grimaced at this additional threat of bodily harm and not wanting his seed to be sucked out of his stalk, continued his plea for more time to come up with the requisite sums, which he had now calculated to be around £1,000, a small amount of which he had collected as stake money.

Having shepherded my team to the middle, I had to recollect where everyone had been standing prior to the cheese ball. I was helped by those who had remembered, Blacky for instance walked to his position at first slip, where wicket-keeper Adam 'Gobshite' Cottrell, was whistling the theme to the movie For A Few Dollars More and looking up towards the trees. Ordinarily Blacky would have rebuked him with some scathing putdown and indeed started before realising that he was in a losing position.

I had decided that I needed to set a more defensive field, even though it was only the third ball of the innings, and dispatched players to all parts of the ground, with particular focus on what had now been dubbed Stilton Corner. Satisfied with my work, I went to chat with Bread who was rolling his arm over and bowling a few looseners.

'Ok Bread?'

'Yes skip.'

'Keep it tight, ok?'

'Yes skip.'

And with the masterful display of captaincy, I walked to my fielding position and awaited the recommencement of play.

Bread Daly came running in to bowl the third ball of an over that had started some 50 minutes previously. The ball landed safely enough, and Paul Pritchard decided that he wasn't going to test his mother's patience a second time and declined to play a shot, letting the ball nestle safely in the gloves of Gobshite Cottrell.

Whilst I was happy with that outcome, I was also not sure what I should do next. The last time I had encouraged the bowler, the ball had disappeared as previously described. So instead, I clapped quietly hoping that this would be sufficient to keep his enthusiasm up. This impasse continued to the end of the over, with the batter wishing to remain part of his family's legacy and the bowler too scared to attempt anything extravagant. It was then a bored umpire Stan who called an end to proceedings and marched the 22 yards to await the next instalment of this unusual game of cricket.

I stood in the middle of the pitch, stroking my chin and vigorously rubbing the ball on my trousers, not a task for the faint hearted. Ordinarily I would have bowled Winners at this stage, as it is traditional for your two quickest bowlers to open the attack, but sensing an opportunity, I opted instead to call Blacky over.

'Right,' I said, 'let's put the betting shenanigans behind us and focus on the job at hand. I want you to prop this end up and keep things tight.'

'Righto skip,' said the suddenly genial WOC, sensing an opportunity to redeem himself. And with that he took the ball from me, marched towards umpire Clarke, threw his cap and jumper at the hapless custodian, who was in the middle of helping the BT batter with his guard taking and ground scratching routine, and marked out his ten-pace run, topping it off with an enthusiastic skip and jump. Umpire Stan, having regained his sight by disentangling himself from Blacky's jumper and readjusting his spectacles, looked around the field to ensure that everyone was ready and indicated that play was to commence.

I have told you about WOCs before and Gordon Blackwell is a WOC of the truest order. He sensed that the BT batters would want to finish this match as quickly as possible, and for them to do so, he would need to position the ball within their striking range. He also realised that if the ball was within said range, then it was likely to meet the same fate as its predecessor and so he decided on a cunning plan worthy of the highest of the highest WOCs.

'Got a plan skip. I'm going to bowl as slowly and as widely as legally possible and, occasionally, throw in a quicker straighter one to fox 'em.'

I know extraordinarily little about bowling, so I nodded in agreement and strolled to my fielding position.

The prey in his sights was, in this case, a young whippersnapper who had been given the Saturday off from the local public school. The first ball was what Blacky would call his quicker ball, but to the batter it was eminently hittable, and he neatly clipped it towards me and jogged to the other end. The bowler was less than pleased and harrumphed loudly mid-pitch, as his whole strategy had been to bowl to the young 'un and leave big-hitting Paul to someone else. Instead, the little bugger had spoiled his plans by taking a single off the very first ball and exposing the WOC to the batter he had planned to avoid.

Blacky walked slowly back to his bowling mark cursing me not having the foresight to realise that the ball would be hit ten feet to my right, nor the athleticism to sprint the required distance and hurl the ball to the wicketkeeper. Bowlers, I thought, are seldom willing to accept that the ball they bowled was a poor one, and more likely to blame the nearest fielder for not anticipating their every move.

Still chuntering, Blacky started to run in and bowled a straight ball to Paul, who had decided that a quick finish was required and proceeded to hit the ball high over the bowler's head and into the trees.

'Oh bloody hell, hide the cheddar,' shouted Jez 'Posh Spice' Dunstan, running leisurely towards the trees, wanting to show willing but not actually be the one to delve into the undergrowth and retrieve the offending object. The standard behaviour when searching for a lost ball is to start off running reasonably quickly and then slow down, hoping that someone else would get there first. But this time, his strategy was flawed as no-one else had bothered running and he was the clear leader in a one-horse race, as it were. Luckily enough, after evading a couple of stray branches, he found the ball and, after checking that he was out of the view of the fielders, he bashed it a few times against the trunk of the nearest tree.

A bit like a golfer in the rough, who kicks his ball a few inches to the right of the bush hoping that no-one will notice, cricketers perform a task called 'scuffing up the ball' to encourage it to behave differently in the hands of their skilled bowler thus giving the fielding team an advantage. In the professional game this has been taken to extreme lengths, with players using materials such as sandpaper to alter the state of the ball. The key phrase to note here is 'skilled bowler' and the plan of knocking dents out of the ball was to give Gordon

Blackwell a chance of removing Big Hitting Paul and his pals.

I started to wander over, slowly mind you, towards where Posh Spice had gone foraging, only for him to emerge from the bushes looking rather smug. He jogged over to a troubled Blacky and slyly showed him the ball.

'Here you go,' whispered the perpetrator, 'the ball hit the trees pretty hard and looks like there are some dents you could use.'

Gordon Blackwell studied the ball carefully and looked in particular at the large indentation just to the left of the seam, or it could be to the right, depending on how you were holding the ball. He turned to the beaming culprit and nodded slowly, understanding the subterfuge that had taken place in the undergrowth.

'Come on lads, we have lost enough time as it is,' chided umpire Stan, adding that he had things to do, beers to drink etc.

'Righto Stan,' replied Gordon, as he gave the ball one last polish and started to trot, with increased intent, towards the crease.

CHAPTER 8 – THE RUMPUS

Big Hitting Paul was getting increasingly frustrated by the slow nature of the game and, whilst he had very little to do later that evening, save maybe ingratiating himself with his parents, he did want to get this match over with as soon as possible. Therefore he decided that regardless of where the next ball landed, he was going to try and hit it as hard and far as he could. Blacky, who was of the same opinion regards the ending of the match, given the suspect device that he was currently fiddling with, ran up and delivered the ball, having craftily positioned it with the dent facing down, hoping for it to deviate dramatically upon landing. He was not to be disappointed.

I watched as he delivered this subterfuge, wondering what the whispering between him and Posh Spice had been about. The ball pitched about three feet away from the batter, who took an almighty swing with every intention of hitting it as far into the trees as he could. However, WOCs are WOCs and can inject cunning into the most benign of deliveries, especially when one is in possession of a dented ball. Therefore, when this haunted and broken object hit the ground, it took a 30º detour to the batter's right and, instead of hitting the middle of Big Hitting Paul's bat, as he had expected, it hit the outside edge instead and flew up and backwards towards a still sulking Bread Daly.

'Catch it Bread,' I yelled, but the fielder was already alert to this requirement and steadied himself as the wayward object came hurtling towards him. Luckily, he did not have to move an inch as he was perfectly positioned, by me I may add, and snaffled the ball cleanly, holding it aloft, to the delight of his teammates.

Even though I was the one who had shouted 'catch it,' I have always found this to be a very strange instruction. Virtually every fielder, especially the bowler, yells this at the person towards whom the ball is flying. I am fairly sure that the redundancy of this call is rooted in the fact that the fielder knows what he is supposed to do. It's not like you need to remind a chicken to lay an egg. I mean they know, right.

We all ran to Bread to congratulate him, whilst Big Hitting Paul was less pleased with the outcome as he trudged off to the sound of us celebrating his dismissal with calls of 'glad we got the slogger out.' He had felt in good form and had hoped to take his team to victory, but he also knew that the next batter, Biffa Jackson, would be able to do just that.

Biffa was an established citizen of Buntingford Smedley and was well-known to some of the older members of the cricket club, as he used to play for us a few seasons ago and remained friends with both me and the Stevens brothers, Flash and Sam. He was well regarded in local cricketing circles as being another hard-hitter and one not to be taken lightly, especially after around 10pm on a Saturday when The Prickly Oyster was moving into fifth gear.

'Alright Biffa,' proffered Flash from his fielding position as his friend and current opponent walked past him.

'Yeh mate, gonna get this over quickly and we can go for a pint,' came the ever-professional answer.

Biffa scratched his guard and took up position, not before asking Gobshite whether that itch had subsided yet, leading to some acute and embarrassed shuffling by our wicketkeeper. He had come to the crease with advice from his team to get on with proceedings and he intended to do exactly that. He looked up at Gordon Blackwell, who seemed to be taking a suspiciously long time in positioning the ball in his chubby hands. Eventually the portly WOC trundled in and produced another eminently hittable delivery that Biffa just prodded into the ground in front of him and picked up the ball.

'Oi what's this then, he asked accusatorially, holding the offending item up for umpire Stan to see. 'Look here Stan, ball's got a bloody great hole in it, how did that 'appen then?'

Gordon had been quick to recover the ball from Bread after he had taken the catch to dismiss Big Hitting Paul Pritchard. Rules of the game dictate that he should have thrown the ball back to Stan Clarke at that stage, but he had noticed that the umpire had temporarily left the field to relieve himself of the liquid that he had consumed during the cheese debacle. Consequently, he had kept the damaged ball to himself, and I was therefore blissfully oblivious to its condition.

It came then as a major surprise to me when Biffa made his accusations, causing yet another hold-up in the day's proceedings. I walked towards the middle of the pitch where an emergency conference between the batter and umpire had started to take place.

I reached the epicentre of events and saw that Biffa had passed the offending article to umpire Clarke, who was turning it over slowly, examining it from every available angle. He eventually held it up to the light, as if expecting some sort of divine intervention, and pointed out the large dent.

'Look at this skipper,' he started with authority, 'this ball has been badly damaged, and I can only assume that your bowler, Blacky, knew about it. You, or he, or both should have told me that the ball was out of condition and that it needed changing. It is simply not on that he, you, or both did not do so.'

And warming to his theme he continued, 'a batter, in this case Paul Pritchard, has had his innings cut short, curtailed I may add, by unfair means and I have half a mind to call him back.'

'You have half a mind full stop,' I thought but instead said 'ok Stan, let me have a look.' This was a vain attempt to buy some time and Biffa knew it.

'Come on Baz, play fair, what is there to look at?' he asked, 'the ball's been done, and Blacky 'ere knew about it. Paul wasn't out mate, you need to call him back as Stan 'ere said.'

This whole calling back business is one that tests the captaincy of a fellow. Essentially this is how it works. If a captain thinks that the batter is not out, even though the umpire has given him out, he can ask the batter to come back and continue his innings. In other words, the umpire's word is not final.

Winning is winning, but doing so by unfair means in the circles of village cricket is something that is harder to shift than the stink of ripe Stilton. A cold shoulder would be given in The Prickly Oyster, Mohammed Ibrahim the proprietor himself of the Taj Mahal Indian restaurant would find you a table near the toilets, if he found you one at all and Jane would be subjected to hostile looks at her yoga class. Overall life would be unbearable, but thankfully I had tackled this thorny subject in my SADFUC document and knew exactly what I should do.

I held the ball in my left hand and studied the indentation that had been created a few moments earlier. I looked at Gordon Blackwell, who was looking nonplussed at events and at my team, who were finding fascination in their fingernails. It was then that I noticed that Posh Spice was shuffling from foot to foot and looking rather sheepish. Sensing that we had a situation on our hands, I beckoned the team to come over to a spot about ten yards away from the irate umpire and batters, who had been joined by their skipper Chris Dingle.

'Lads, truth time - what have we done? Have we scuffed this ball, have we cheated?' I asked, adding 'Jez, you found the ball, what state was it in?'

Jez 'Posh Spice' Dunstan looked up, wishing now that he had just thrown the ball back to Blacky and stammered 'well Baz, you know, well I' but he was interrupted by a belligerent Gordon Blackwell.

'Listen lads, ball got dented when their bloke smashed it into the trees, end of. Let's just say that it is a cricketing matter and that we didn't think that the ball was too damaged.'

I stared at the unrepentant WOC whilst consulting the imaginary SADFUC document that I memorised through nightly reading, to the annoyance of Jane who had asked why 'I couldn't just read a murder-mystery like a normal person.' I quickly found the 'brand of cricket' section and located the sub-section that confirmed that we would uphold the laws of the game.

'Leaders are born, not made Barry' I told myself and, ignoring my teammates, I marched up to umpire Clarke, gave him the ball and said, in a

155

strong and unfaltering voice

'Stan, we should have told you that the ball is in an unfit condition, for which we apologise, and we would like to call the last batter back.'

'Quite right skipper,' intoned the umpire, relieved that he would not have to deal with an ugly situation.

'Good decision Bazza,' said Biffa, 'I'll let you buy me a beer after for that.' And with that, he walloped on the shoulder, causing me to lose a bit of balance and dislodge a bit of cheese from the waistband of my trousers

Not everyone thought that I had made a good decision though. Gordon Blackwell, not the most composed and balanced of human beings at the best of time, came as close to internally, and probably externally, combusting as he had ever come. He stormed over to me, Biffa and Stan and was just about to let forth his views on the subject of calling batters back and sodding manifestos when the umpire stopped him.

'Further to the laws of the game, I am awarding five penalty runs to Bishop's Tackle and banning Gordon Blackwell from bowling again in this match.'

And with that he moved to the side and asked Chris Dingle to bring Paul Pritchard back to resume his innings. Little did umpire Stan Clarke realise that he had just started a chain reaction of events that would have lasting consequences.

Gordon Blackwell roared a series of expletives that had left the wide-eyed young BT batter making a mental note for future use in school and, having pushed the Dingle to the floor, he near enough strangled Stan Clarke by ripping his sweater off the neck of the hapless umpire and stormed off towards the pavilion. Forty pairs of eyes, including those of Dave the dog, followed this unexpected turn of events with a combination of horror and sheer fascination and watched as the irate WOC blustered into our changing rooms, packed up his kit, stormed out towards his car, fired up its engine and screeched out of the car park.

'He'll do anything to not pay his debts,' said Gilo somewhat unhelpfully, but with comic timing.
This had been a stern, early test for my SADFUC manifesto and, whilst it had provided me with the moral compass to call the batter back, the sad truth of the matter was that on day one of my new dawn, my team was down to nine men and, more pertinently, only three proper bowlers.

I had not moved an inch during the entire episode and had watched the WOC storm off with mixed feelings. Some members of the team, namely Sam and Flash had made a vain attempt to get him to change his mind, but as the majority had little or no time for the saviour of Britain, they did little apart from shake their heads and shrug their shoulders. Nine men or not, the game would be more enjoyable now.

Paul Pritchard had had the misfortune to happen to pass Blacky as he made his way back onto the pitch.

'You tell your Dad I won't be buying his cheeses ever again.'

'Uh ok Uncle Gordon, I'll tell him.'

Even though Gordon Blackwell was the sister of Ma P, the mother of the Pritchard family, and therefore Paul was his nephew, the incoming batter had taken the precaution of giving the seething former bowler a wide berth just in case he became the object of any familial retribution. Nephew Paul had just reached the middle when Biffa slung his bat over his shoulder and started to walk merrily off the pitch.

'That's my job done then, nought not out. You two crack on and I'll see you in the bar,' he said and continued his journey back to the pavilion, regally waving at imaginary fans, to await the applause of his jubilant teammates.

Big Hitting Nephew Paul was somewhat sheepish upon his return to the crease and did not waste much time scratching a new guard and suchlike. He merely tapped the ground a few times and looked up, waiting for the bowler to start his run up. Except there was no bowler.

With all the shenanigans taking place, I had totally forgotten that someone else would need to bowl the rest of Blacky's over. In a bit of a panic, I wandered over to chat with Winners and Bread.

'Bread, do you fancy this end?' I asked, before realising that he had just finished at the other and so couldn't bowl the remainder of this over.

'Winners, what about you?'

'Could do skip but would need to warm up first in case

I do myself a mischief. Why doesn't some else bowl the rest of this one and I can warm up first?'

Whilst I was arranging these logistics, umpire Clarke's mood was worsening by the second, and having already given Bishop's Tackle five extra runs for the dented ball incident, he was in the mood for more.

'Skipper,' he squeaked in a tone an octave or two higher than normal, 'if you don't get on with this ruddy game, I will award Bishop's Tackle five runs for every minute delayed.'

'You can't do that,' said Winners, 'there is nothing in the laws about how long we take.'

'Listen chap,' replied Stan, adjusting his collar to allow the built-up steam to escape, 'I don't bloody care if it's in the bloody laws. GET ON WITH THE SODDING GAME.'
This last outburst prompted a 'ooooh' from Gilo who simultaneously lifted his hands up, vertical to his chest to indicate that Stan should have been holding a handbag

'Right, that's it, an extra five runs to BT for time wasting and insubordination towards a standing official,' and with that umpire Clarke walked five paces to his right and held up his hand to show the scorers that he had awarded five extra runs to the batting side.

'Woh, woh, woh Stan,' I said, 'you can't do that, and you know you can't. Yes, we were deciding who to bowl, but that situation was somewhat forced upon by....'

'by Blacky buggering off with our cash.' interrupted Gilo, unhelpfully, but did elicit guffaws from the team.

'This is your final, final warning,' said the now dangerously out of control umpire, 'if you don't bowl the ball in the next minute, I will do the same again.'

I was not going to let this jumped-up, ex-bank manager-cum-third-rate umpire who was two and a half pints of bitter in, throw his weight around without exercising my right to reply as captain.

'Stan,' I tried soothingly, 'let's all calm down and discuss.....'

'Five more runs to Bishop's Tackle,' said the tyrant-cum-umpire as he marched, five outstretched fingers held high, ten yards to his left, where he bumped into the mountainous figure of Gilo Aikens who had uprooted one of the stumps and was currently holding it across his chest in a menacing fashion.

'Now then Stan,' Gilo said, slowly and ominously for effect, 'stop with your bloody five runs obsession, go back to your position and get ready to umpire the next bleedin' ball, or I will insert this stump up your jacksie.'

Stan Clarke adjusted his spectacles which had been dislodged, again, by the impact with Gilo's caveman-like frame and decided, probably sensibly, that acquiescence was a better option and walked slowly backwards to his position, his eye never leaving the stump.

I breathed a sigh of relief at Gilo's intervention and mouthed a 'thank you' at him, to which he responded by blowing me back a kiss, causing Gobshite to redden.

'Good work Gilo, now can you put the stump back so we can crack on like,' he said after recovering his composure.

Gilo rammed the stump back in and took up his position of both second and third slip and waited for the bowler that I, in the middle of the mayhem, had chosen to complete the over.

Now, I didn't really bowl, apart from in the nets, and even then, it was very occasionally. But I did not want to waste any of the main bowler's overs as they only had ten each and so decided to bowl the few couple of balls myself and then turn to Winners as he had suggested. I can't bring myself to describe in these pages what these deliveries were like, suffice to say that the young 'un took great delight in despatching my efforts to all parts of the ground. I was truly thankful when I collected my cap and jumper from a nervous umpire to retire to my fielding position, vowing never to bowl again.

At this stage, if anyone is interested in the score, it was 30-0 off 12 legal balls and a wide and had taken just over an hour.

The rest of the match continued at a pace much subdued from the previous and the batters wasted no time in thrashing our bowlers all over the Bishop's Tackle ground. I had put one of our younger bowlers on for a change and with his spin and cunning changes of pace, he had given us some glimmer of hope by taking the wickets of the Young 'Un, the returning Biffa, the Dingle and a couple of other BT batters. But Big Hitting Paul was holding firm and, when he pushed a leg stump ball from Bread between Sam and Flash for a single, he gave a shout of delight and held his bat in the air to signal he had reached 50 runs. The score at this stage was 102-5.

As a bit of a traditionalist, I have always enjoyed the old school ways and raising one's bat when one reaches 50 or 100 is a time-honoured practice. I had read in Wisden that this may have started as a way of a batter showing their appreciation to the crowd, who were busy applauding politely and throwing their bowler hats in the air. The tradition still exists, with the headwear replaced by plastic beer glasses, but why it exists at club level is a bit of a mystery to me, after all there is virtually no crowd and just a smattering of applause from your team.

'50-1' shouted Gobshite for all to hear, referring to the fact that the batter had already been out once and shouldn't have been there at all.

'Shouldn't have bloody cheated then should you,' retorted Biffa, in his latest role as square-leg umpire.

Adam 'Gobshite' Cottrell was not known for his cognitive skills and certainly had not heard of, let alone practiced, any form of mindfulness. His only association with this practice was leaving The Prickly Oyster after only four pints, with sufficient mental faculties to remember to visit Kebab Korner on his way home. So when Biffa had come back with this comment, added to the earlier jibe about his personal habits, the chimp in Gobshite's mind went into overdrive and started screeching about the insult to both his and the team's character.

Not for the first time in an afternoon's match of village cricket, I stood and watched in horror as my carefully planned SADFUC strategy collapsed around me. Rather than shaking his head and letting it pass, Gobshite took off his gloves and ran towards Biffa, having uprooted the same stump that Gilo had waved at the umpire a little earlier.

It is generally accepted that there are two distinct courses of action taken by the bystanders during times like this. The first is to stand still in shock and disbelief and the second is to run towards the rumpus. There is also a crossover, where the person who initially undertakes the option A, then takes Option B but is more likely to nervously hover around the periphery. We had a mixture of all three as Gobshite started on his suicide mission.

I had known Biffa since primary school and he had been the biggest in our class by far, and by the time he was 12 he was taller than a couple of teachers. He earned his nickname when he was about 19 because of his dual abilities to wallop the cricket ball very hard as well as hitting people equally as firmly, especially after a few pints of Sniper's Snakepit in The Prickly Oyster. When you are well over 6 feet in height and weigh in at 150 kilos, the impact of your blow upon both the ball and the chin of an opponent is keenly felt by both. So when he saw our diminutive wicketkeeper running towards him, fury burning in his eyes, Biffa was more than a touch amused.

As were the 75%, who took the opportunity to exercise both their legs and their vocal cords and were currently running towards the scene of the impending crime.

Chris Dingle and I had both run towards the scene as soon as Gobshite had started his sprint towards Biffa, with me getting there first given I was a lot closer to start with. I had tried to grab him before he reached Biffa, but I was too late and arrived just as he swung the stump as hard as he could towards his opponent, who caught it in a giant paw and ripped it out of a stunned Gobshite's hand. Biffa threw it to the ground and grabbed the offending wicketkeeper by the throat.

'Listen you little...'

He had just started to describe Gobshite accurately when he was cut down by a rugby tackle from Flash Stevens, who had been a useful fly half in his time. All three ended up in a heap on the floor and were soon joined by a dozen others from both sides, who had joined the melee to relieve their boredom.

'Lads, lads come on this is a game of cricket, its not bloody rugby,' I pleaded, whilst simultaneously frantically scanning my SADFUC document for guidance.

"Yeh fellas, that's enough,' agreed the Dingle whilst trying to retrieve one or two of his players from the ruck

With fists flying and protagonists being thrown

out of the to-do, only to jump back in again, the sight was a strange one. People show their true colours in times like and, whilst you would have thought that Gilo would have been at the centre of the fuss, he was instead stretched out comfortably, chewing on a blade of grass, a good 10 feet away from the action, in conversation with Sam Stevens and Winners.

'Look at that silly old sod,' he stated, referring to umpire Stan's vain attempt at regaining control. 'How does he think that clapping his hands like a scout master and shouting 'come on boys' is going to help?' he asked.

'Bloody embarrassing,' said Sam, adding 'it's not even a proper fight, just handbags and knob rubbing.'

'Knob rubbing,' laughed Winners, 'that private school education is shining through there mate.'

'Hah no way pal, look at them thrashing about like a bunch of choirboys in the shower after singsong,' Sam retorted.

Winners thought about repeating the same public school jibe, but instead Gilo brought a much-needed sense of urgency to the situation by shouting over to me.

'Oi Baz. Get a grip son, if this goes on for much longer the bloody pub will be shut. And if I can't get a drink after this bollocks of a day there will be a fight, I can tell you.'
The dissenting 25%, who were also lounging about on the grass watching the commotion, laughed but also turned to me in the hope that I would show some leadership.

I took a deep breath and a step back from the fracas, put the thumb and forefinger of my left hand to my mouth and emitted a loud, ear-piercing whistle. In an instant, I had single-handedly brought the battle of Bishop's Tackle to a mid-punch halt.

After I had brought an end to proceedings, the Dingle and I agreed that we should have an impromptu drinks break, after which the game could continue and so it did, with the ball flying to all corners of the ground until such a point where BT's score passed ours. This was only 25 minutes after the final bell, Paul Pritchard finished on 72 not out and was righty applauded off the pitch, as is the tradition, followed by the rest of the protagonists. Flash and Biffa, who had last been seen rolling around on the floor together, walked off bruised but still laughing at their behaviour whilst Gobshite made sure that he was a long way behind.

The BT chair rose to make a speech about the sort of behaviour that he and the rest of the committee had just witnessed, found deplorable and that we had brought the local game into disrepute. He would, he said, be making a formal complaint to the league's secretary and sending our chair, The Badger, a strongly worded note. With that he coughed violently and sat back down in his deck chair, exhausted by his efforts.
I couldn't lay any blame at the door of the Bishop's Tackle set-up and said so to the Dingle.

'Bloody nightmare that Chris.'

'Yeh not exactly the way that I thought today would go. I had wanted balls to be flying all over the shop, but hadn't expected the same for lumps of cheese and fists,' he said shaking his head, adding, 'fancy a pint?

All of the heroes of our story, having shaken hands and packed up our kit bags, assembled in the bar area of the BT clubhouse to chat about the day's events and congratulate Paul Pritchard on his match-winning innings.

I walked to the corner of the bar where Stan Clarke was on his own, sitting in an armchair with his pint of beer on the table beside him. He was leaning forwards, with his hands covering his face and, as I approached him, he looked up at me with one bespectacled eye and started moaning and rocking slowly. I think he may have started crying.

I about-turned swiftly and walked back to the crowd surrounding Big Hitting Paul, who was pouring them all beer from his celebratory jug.

'Thanks for the game Chris and all the best for the rest of the season,' I said insincerely.

'Cheers Baz, hope it's less eventful than today.

I then turned to Flash and Gobshite and told them that I was going to head back to The Wreck, and if they wanted a lift they needed to come now.

And so started the mass exodus of our players from the warmth of the BT clubhouse to the impending fire greeting us back at The Wreck.

CHAPTER 9 - THE COURT CASE

The drive from the village of Bishop's Tackle to The Wreck seemed to go a lot quicker than the journey that we had undertaken that morning, not surprising given that I wasn't expecting anything but a frosty reception when we arrived.

This being the modern age, news of the riotous scenes that had taken place at Bishop's Tackle had reached the good people of Buntingford Smedley CC before any of us had made an appearance. And when the three of us in the advance battalion walked into the bar-cum-tearoom, we found the full complement of the second and third teams, plus The Badger, Doug and Dave the dog awaiting our return.

The crowd was unusually large, those who would have ordinarily gone straight home after a match, or would bypass The Wreck for The Prickly Oyster, had ripped up their usual plans and had assembled within, awaiting the development of a scenario more akin to an episode of Eastenders than Buntingford Smedley CC.

'Umm right ho,' I stuttered, 'good, umm turn out.'

'How did you get on today?' I asked Hawk, the first person that I saw upon entering.

'We got hammered mate, but I think you'll find that your match will be the subject of every conversation tonight'

I didn't doubt it but wanted to delay proceedings at least until the rest of the team had arrived and I some back up. The thought hit me that may swerve supporting me and go to The Pricky Oyster or worse still, go straight home and hide.

The Badger was looking particularly annoyed, his reputation at the Conservative Club, Buntingford Smedley Bowling Club and the parish council amongst others was probably at stake and, I suspected that if he didn't deal with this situation effectively, there was the real threat that committees would sit and either deliver a stern rebuke or would be actively considering banishing him from their midst.

He had gone into the corner of the room, a frown

on his usually even tempered, tanned face and was talking to his brother, Noodle.

'I need your support in this. When the rest of that bloody shower show their faces, I will haul Barry and his team over the coals. I must show Major Foxton-Bossington that I am a force to be reckoned with, remember that it's the parish council presidential elections next week, and he can't win. Campbell family pride is at stake.'

Noodle nodded in agreement, turned and scowled at me to demonstrate that the brothers were united and meant business.

I later learned that news of the incident had reached The Badger, via a text from Doug that read 'ball in cheese, scrap on pitch.' Apparently, he hadn't been entirely sure what to make of it, nor whether the two parts had any connection to each other, even though they were in the same sentence. He had wondered whether Doug had meant that there was a scrap of cheese on the pitch but then wondered why Doug was telling him. As he couldn't think of any reasons, he concluded that Doug had inadvertently sent him the message. He was soon put right by the next text from Noodle, who had written 'bloody disgrace, the first team have been fighting on the pitch. You need to deal with this and remove Barry from the captaincy. DEAL WITH IT.'

I didn't know any of this on the evening in question, but I did know that I was in some serious strife, and that this could be the shortest captaincy in the club's history. The door opened and I was relieved to see Flash, Sam and Bread enter the bar-cum-tearoom followed by Winners and the rest of the team. Their way to the bar was blocked by the large number of people in attendance who were staring at them, some with mouths agog and some with a knowing smirk. The mood at The Wreck was deliciously polarised between the fervent and the furious.

The crowd started to bombard the unprepared rearguard with a volley of questions.

'What the hell happened?'

'Gobshite did you start it you knobber?'

'Does Bazza still smell of cheese?'

I could have answered that last question myself and was about to do so when I was summoned to attend a private chat with The Badger in his self-ordained Chair's Corner.

'At least let me get a drink,' I said, feeling that I was going to need at least one.

'Quickly then,' replied The Badger, adding, 'and get me one.'

Unfortunately, Noodle was tending the bar that evening and my request for two pints of his best bitter was met with a fierce glare, followed by a begrudging pouring of pints and, unable to control himself, a lecture.

'Bloody disgrace, really you are, you've brought this club into disrepute, and on the first match of the season too, Lord knows what the remainder will be like. There again you may not be there to find out. You've always lacked leadership qualities Barry, and this is what happens. We need to bring back National Service to make sure it doesn't happen again.'
I stood bemused, wondering whether there was a chance that this had been blown out of all proportion.

'Thanks Noodle, you're a credit to your family and society.'

I paid for the beers, ignoring Noodle's not so subtle hints that I should buy him a drink as part of my penance and walked, head held high to the area where The Badger was located.

This Chair's Corner is what The Badger had alluded

to in his speech at the AGM and was a snug area with a single red lounge chair and a smaller beige number, both of which The Badger had transported from his house. Adjacent to the larger chair was a small, unhappy-looking side table upon which stood a lamp with a cricket ball shaped shade, a 'Reserved' sign from the Taj Mahal Indian restaurant next to which was a specially made one, that indicated that the space was indeed he badger's den and for his official use only.

I gave our leader his beer and took my place in the beige chair, awaiting my fate. He had intended for this to be a private tete-a-tete between the club chair and first team captain during which he would lay down certain expectations of behaviour both on and off the pitch and how I, Barry, had fallen way short of these expectations leaving he, The Badger, with a tough decision to make.

But the bar-cum-tearoom at The Wreck is a 1970s open room and featured four magnolia walls with pictures of the various teams who had represented Buntingford Smedley over the years, including a youthful Badger and a middle-aged Doug with Dave the puppy. Interspersed were plaques and the very occasional trophies that represented success in the eyes of the leaders of the club. With these architectural constraints and a low artexed ceiling with a central light bulb cased in another cricket-ball shaped shade, the chances of a private hearing were precisely zero.

I settled back in my chair, aware of the fact that this was going to be a public trial and that the gallery was made up of the members of the three teams, partners, officials and a dog. All of them, Dave included, were hanging onto The Badger's every word.

'Good evening gentlemen, ah and lady,' he started.

'And dog,' shouted Gobshite, who was immediately cuffed round the head by Biffa.

'You've caused enough problems today you little git. Baz is in the dock because of you.'

'Um thank you Biffa,' continued The Badger, 'this is an official disciplinary hearing under Law 42, Players' Conduct don't you know, in the Marylebone Cricket Club laws and that, given it was a level 4 offence, Barry should be entitled to an attorney. But as we don't have one, well then, he can go without.'

The crowd emitted a low hum of approval in respect of The Badger's knowledge of the laws of the game, but I was left looking slightly puzzled at this official turn of events and scanned the room for someone who was foolhardy enough to defend my actions during both the cheese debacle and the on-field dust up.

Those who had not been at Bishop's Tackle that day were eagerly looking around the bar-cum-tearoom to see where I would get my advocacy from, and those who were there were avoiding any eye contact with me.

Not put off by my team's apparent lack of support, I put my index fingers to my lips as I had seen barristers on the TV do and made my choice.

'I appoint Winners as my advocate.'

'Oh bollocks,' he responded when he heard me call his name out, 'couldn't you have called Flash to represent you, after all he was the closest?'

'Flash was definitely the closest, he was in the middle of the blooming ruck,' explained Gobshite, then quickly realising he had incriminated his opening batter.

He tried to retract his statemen by adding 'but he was only trying to stop Biffa walloping me.'

'I don't know why I bothered you little scrote,' countered Flash Stevens to laughter from the crowd who were thoroughly looking forward to the next hour or so. At my expense, no doubt.

With this as his backdrop, Winners had decided that he needed to take his newly elevated position seriously, and that he had to at least look the part of a Queen's Counsel. He excused himself and returned with an old mop head that he had found in the cleaner's storeroom, which he placed on his head and turned to address the gallery.

'QC Simon Winston in da house and I is here to defend Mr Barry Compton Briggs and that his honour the judge The Badger isn't to take no liberties.' Noodle tutted loudly and muttered something about the blatant misuse of the Queen's language by those from the colonies.

The courtroom, on the other hand, found this impromptu disguise wholly appropriate and signalled their satisfaction with cheering and applause. Flash decided that further embellishment was required and whipped the black cloth off the pool table and suggested that Winners used this as a gown.

'Top work Flash, don the cloak Winners,' shouted Sam.

With a flourish, my attorney swirled the cloak around his shoulders, adjusted his headgear and, now suitably attired, sat on the stool he had been given by Bread.

'I is now ready m'lud, you may commence proceedings against my client, B. Briggs esquire.'
The Badger, not amused by this barefaced disregard for his authority, stood up to calm the boisterous gallery who were thoroughly enjoying this unexpected Saturday night's entertainment.

'Winners remove that bloody mop head and pool table cover and start to take things seriously.

'Spoilsport, I was role playing Badg,' but nonetheless he returned from renegade QC to plain old Simon 'Winners' Winston, I was not sure which one I preferred.
After some order had been resumed, The Badger opened proceedings.

'Barry we are assembled here today' then had to stop immediately as the crowd started howling with laughter asking if The Badger had morphed into the Reverend Pondswell.

'This is an important meeting guys, something that has consequences for both the club and the community, so if you're not going to take things seriously, please sod off and do something else,' he barked.

'Consequences for your chances of being elected as councillor you mean,' muttered Whitey, drawing a stern glare from both Noodle and the Badger.

'I will choose to ignore that slur Whitey,' The Badger gallantly countered, making a mental note to speak with him privately later to explain how he would be the best candidate for the post. Instead, he paused, stood, held the lapels of his green tweed jacket with his thumbs and forefingers and started proceedings.

'Buntingford Smedley has a very good local reputation, both as a village and a cricket club, one that has been rightly earned over a number of years and I, as chair, will not stand to one side and see it sullied, yes sullied, by events such as today's kerfuffle. As captain of the first team Barry, could you please factually explain what occurred and what actions, remedial or otherwise, you took to ensure the aforesaid reputation of the club remained intact.'

A few junior members of the club as well as Whitey and his wife Lorraine looked a trifle bemused at the language flowing eloquently from their chair's mouth, but the orator was in full flight and rather pleased with his handling of the situation to date.

'You must all know that I only have the club's best interests, and only that at heart, and that any personal feelings and positions in the community will be put firmly to one side.'

And with that he sat back down, crossed his legs, flicked some imaginary crumbs off his fawn-coloured chinos and took a long draught of his beer.

The crowd appeared satisfied with The Badger's efforts, and silence descended in the bar-cum-tearoom as all eyes then turned to me, the accused and Winners my attorney, now devoid of accessories.

I rose from my seat, remembering the Ted Talk on leadership that I had had with Darren Perkins and, quite possibly because of the memory of that encounter, I sat down again and addressed both the chair and the crowd.

'Well this is a tale worthy of the finest TV dramas like Midsomer Murders, Death in Paradise and Morse', I started.

'Death in Paradise is rubbish and shouldn't be included mate. The other two yes, but not that.'
Gobshite's interjection resulted in a short, but fierce debate on the pros and cons of the various programmes with other suggestions such as Agatha Raisin and Jonathan Creek thrown in for balance.

An exasperated Badger slammed his fist on the unhappy looking round side table, which promptly collapsed causing the table light with the cricket ball shade and his beer glass to crash to the floor, stopping the TV drama discussion in its tracks, which was the intended outcome.

'CAN we please get on,' he shouted whilst looking for someone to come and clear up the mess he had created, and followed with 'and bring me another pint please, I'll settle up later.'

I looked at the broken glass, remnants of the table and lamp and wasted beer and realised that angering The Badger again would lead to my own downfall and that a factual approach would be better. With this in mind, I related the day, starting with the broken toe suffered by Chocks Tillwell, the cheese incident in its ripest glory, the wager and disappearance of Blacky with cash, the ball tampering and the on-field ruck. I left no stone unturned; it was detail personified.

The crowd had been remarkably quiet during my discourse save a few 'ooohs' and 'aaahs' and a prolonged 'poooh' when the cheese affair was described and, when I had finished, they broke into a round of applause and beseeched The Badger to forgive the Tiger of Bishop's Tackle who, under trying conditions, had done his best to uphold the best traditions of both the club and the glorious game.

The Badger leaned back and put his finger to his lips, as I had done earlier, and re-furrowed his already furrowed brow. You could cut the tension in The Wreck bar-cum-tearoom-cum-courthouse with a knife as the amassed throng awaited his decision. With a keen sense of occasion, The Badger cleared his throat and was about to deliver his judgement when Whitey decided that he needed to have his say.

He pushed his way through the crowd and came to confront us in the Chairman's Corner. He held his lapels as he had seen the Badger do and spun dramatically to face The Badger.

'May hi hask his honour what was the point of hasking the QC to remove the bog brush from his 'ead, given he was sat there for half an hour doing nuffink but picking his nose?' He asked in an accent that was mock snootiness crossed with your conventional cockney.

The crowd, impressed by Whitey's unlikely reading of the situation, murmured their assent and agreed that Winners' role was wholly unnecessary and that he added nothing to the proceedings.

'Put him in the dock for bring the trial into disrepute,' suggested Gilo from his viewing point at the bar.

'Hang him,' bayed the crowd eager for some sort of retribution, not realising the historical significance of their comments until Sam Stevens pointed it out.

Whitey retired to the comfort of a beaming Lorraine, buoyed by slaps on the back as he passed through the crowd.

'Blimey I try to help and what do I get,' Winners stood grinning and bowed to his audience, eliciting cheers, applause and offers of a drink as he took his place in the throng.

I was unsure which way this would go. On the one hand, I had given a fair account of the day and my role, which had not aggravated any of the situations and, I had also called the batter back, putting our club in a positive light. On the other hand, The Badger wanted to be re-elected as a councillor. It was going to be tight.

The verdict soon came as The Badger rose, a touch unstable after his beer intake and proclaimed that he had come to a decision in the case of the Club v Briggs.

'I have considered the evidence provided and I rule that..' but before he could rule anything there was a voice from the back of the room.

'You've not asked me Badg, me old mucker.' The crowd, not for the first time today ooohed and turned in unison to the voice, which revealed itself as coming from the mouth of Biffa.

'Alright Biffa,' chimed the crowd as one as their one-time teammate and now opponent pushed his way through the crowd to the front of the court and faced The Badger.

'Biffa, firstly you are no longer a member of this club and secondly I am afraid you are too late to have your say,' proclaimed the exasperated chair, 'for having considered the evidence and the stout defence provided by the defendant, I declare Barry Briggs innocent of all charges.'

Upon hearing the declaration of innocence, the crowd cheered, and I let out a long sigh of relief and started to rise from my chair, only to resume contact with it almost immediately as my shoulder made a firm connection with the hand of Biffa, who had made his way to the front of the courtroom.

'I don't think he is,' said the BT player, 'I saw him perform a despicable act and it is time that he was exposed.'

I looked up in puzzlement at my possibly soon to be ex-school friend who, having seen both The Badger and Whitey do so, clasped the non-existent lapels of his dirty t-shirt and cleared his throat.

'M'lud The Honourable Badger, I meself saw the defendant Barry Compton Briggs on the evening of the 12th thereof, walking into The Prickly Oyster, a public house of these here parts, and buy a pint for himself, ignoring the pitiful calls for refreshments from his school friend and a long-standing yeoman brother of this parish, vis a vis, me. For this act of selfishness and today's cheese mithering incident, ruining the livelihood of an upstanding local family, I call upon the assembled masses to pass judgement on Barry Compton Briggs.'

The crowd looked at each other at this unexpected turn of events. Firstly, were they being asked to usurp The Badger and if so, what judgement was Biffa looking for?

All became clear when the chief agitator took up the mantle again.'I declare as the voice of the masses, that Bazza is guilty of the crimes outlined and that the most suitable punishment is that he should stand a round of drinks for the thirsty assembled.'

And with that, Biffa's vast arm, and accompanying odours swept across the room, proclaiming a sound and fair outcome to proceedings and, to make sure that I actioned his pronouncement, he lifted me up and carried me to the bar, accompanied by a crowd delirious with excitement and the prospect of free beer.

I was secretly relieved that I had not been removed as captain of the first team and that I could continue to implement the brand of cricket that I had outlined in my SADFUC document. I smiled broadly at the crowd and proceeded to order a jug each of lager and bitter to complete my punishment, as determined by Biffa. Noodle was still behind the bar, seemingly angrier at the outcome, filled each 5 pint jug with the required liquid and, even though it should have been my honour, Gilo and Biffa took it upon themselves to top up their own glasses and fill up those of the gleeful crowd, all of whom were happy with this provision of free beer, except Lorraine White, who said,

'Ere where's my drink Baz, I don't drink lager.'

I sighed and asked her what she wanted.

'Vodka and orange, make it a large one,' she replied,

adding 'and proper vodka Noodle not your watered down one.'

'Single vodka and orange,' I ordered to a backdrop of a singular cry of 'cheapskate.'

I walked over to The Badger with a fresh pint, straight from the tap, and not from the now empty jug.

'Thanks for your understanding and lenience in the matter mate. You know how much this club and the captaincy mean to me,'
The Badger, pleased with his conduct and how he had passed judgement, nodded his head gracefully and said that he couldn't wish for a better custodian for the club and all that he held dear.

The rest of the evening was reasonably uneventful with the main conversation centring around individual performances across the three teams, a young 'un had scored a half-century on his third team debut and was roundly congratulated, by all except Noodle who had to limit his beer consumption on account of having to drive the youth home. The eager youngster, having observed the traditions of buying a jug for batting or bowling successes had offered to buy one, but given his age, his offer of 5 pints of lemonade was largely vetoed.

The other subject of conversation was that of Blacky and the case of the missing money.

The bar-cum-tearoom was generally up to speed with the circumstances surrounding the cheese incident and the ensuing bet, and so conjecture rested solely on the location of the missing WOC. No man, woman or dog had seen Gordon Blackwell since he stormed out of Bishop's Tackle earlier that afternoon. Calls had been made to his known haunts, which included The Prickly Oyster, Ye Olde Millstone and The Red Lion in the neighbouring village of Castington. All of these returned a negative result as did calls to his mobile and a visit to his home Rumbledown Farm, on the edge of Buntingford.

'I reckon he's Lord Lucaned it,' suggested Gilo, referring to the missing peer of the realm who did his nanny in and legged it with the help of his well-to-do friends. Allegedly.

'Hundred quid's not going to get him sipping champers in Monaco, is it?' ventured Winners.

'Well you'd bloody know wouldn't you,' sniped Whitey who was met with a withering glance from Bread.

'I'll send you a postcard next time I go, you wazzock.'

'Well we would rather go to Clacton, better food and it's more authentic innit,' Lorraine chimed in and received a nod of appreciation from both her husband and Noodle, forgiving her for suggestion that he watered down the vodka.

Before any simmering feud could develop into anything fruitier, The Badger decided that he was still on firm ground after his earlier performance and stepped in with another edict from the echelons of club management. He tapped his glass on the bar to gain everyone's attention.

'I have considered Blacky's actions today and I consider them devious, dastardly and underhand. Therefore, an extraordinary committee sat earlier this evening and decreed that Gordon Blackwell is now a persona non grata within Buntingford Smedley CC and its environs.'

'He means he's been fired Whitey,' Bread explained, in defence of the former's snipe at his friend.
'I know what he meant.'

Expecting a more robust response, the crowd turned to Lorraine White, who considered a night in the cricket club as a night 'out, but not out out.'

'My 'usband and in fact not me neither is stupid and can understand English perfectly well thank you and we don't need no smart arse showing us up.'

With the future of the English language in safe hands, The Badger finished his proclamation with the somewhat unnecessary 'and he will not be selected by any team until he is let back in.' With that he solemnly walked to the bar and asked Noodle to pour him a beer adding that he had no cash and would settle up later.

I convened a group consisting of the remaining members of the first team, all of whom had given money to Blacky.

'Right we need to pull a plan together to find him, get our money back and then convince The Badger to reintegrate him,' I said.

'He's probably gone to a mate's house, assuming he has one, and will turn up in a few days' suggested Winners.

'Yeh we can collar him then,' suggested Gilo, clenching his fists.
Not surprisingly there was not much in the way of concern for the missing WOC, the consensus was that we were better off without him and so my final wish fell on somewhat deaf ears,

I was concerned with the impact Gordon's absence would have on the team and its future selection. I would now be without both of my WOCs for the rest of the season and would need to select two new players for next Saturday. What was worrying me was that Dave 'Whitey' White would almost certainly have to be one of them and that he could single-handedly ruin my SADFUC strategy, just when I had saved it from collapse on its first outing.

Back in the corner, the assembled had decided that we would pay Blacky a visit and demand our money from him en masse. The assumption was that he would be back on his farmstead tomorrow morning, given that the cows wouldn't milk themselves. And with that we shook hands and went our separate ways, which in my case was home to Jane and the kids, who no doubt would be captivated by the day's adventures.

I hadn't realised the time when I put my key into the door of 42 Kingston Road and when I shouted that I was back and had a tale of great hilarity to relate, I was met with darkness and silence. I shook my head at the great let down and vowed to tell everyone the next morning.

And with that I got a beer out of the fridge, wet a cloth from the kitchen and began to clean my bat.

CHAPTER 10 - THE SEARCH

It was Sunday morning, as it was pretty much everywhere up and down this fair isle, and I was at the breakfast table with the family, exhausted but equally elated at the events of yesterday. I was sure that other cricketers would be boring their long-suffering families stiff with monologues on runs, wickets and catches, whereas I had an altogether different tale to tell.

And for once I had the attention of the entire family, Jane included.

'and that is how the ball came out of the cheese,' I concluded before refilling my mug from the teapot. And with that, I moved swiftly on to the story of the bet and how that had led to an increase in tensions, resulting in the rumpus on the pitch.

'Did you fight Uncle Biffa?' asked Ella, noticing that I was unscarred and therefore this question may have been redundant.

'No darling, I didn't fight anyone. And neither should any of you. Fighting with your fists means that you don't have the words to defend yourself and, words are more powerful than guns.' I concluded.

I am sure that I heard Jane sigh as she sensed that something that had started out as a jolly story was going to descend mercilessly into another of my moral lectures.

'Ok dad, I have some questions,' said Ben, who had been making notes throughout my story.

'Not now Ben,' I said, 'I will be out for a couple of hours, we are going to see Blacky and get him to pay us back the winnings from the cheese bet.'

Jane was both surprised and less than impressed by my late admission.

'Barry, really, is that more important than spending some quality time with your children?'

I knew what the correct answer should have been, but sometimes the male mouth moves at a faster speed than the male brain and I really should have just agreed with her and stayed in.

'Yeh but I told the lads I would be there, and I am their captain after all.

Knowing that I had got it wrong again, I avoided Jane's stare, which was transmitting thoughts of what on earth she had seen in me all those years ago and thinking, wrongly, that I was on safe ground, I gave her a peck on the cheek and a solemn promise to do something with them in the afternoon.

We had arranged to meet at The Sacred Scone Cafe at 10am and I arrived at five minutes before the appointed time to see that the nine first eleven players who had played in the match, along with Biffa, were already there.

'Morning lads.'

'Alright Baz, want a coffee?'

'No I'm good thanks,' I said continuing the gripping chat.

Biffa and Gilo were making short work of their full English, with beans and egg furiously dispersing themselves about the small table that they were occupying.

'Good nosh, I needed that after yesterday's lock-in.'

'Isn't that your second breakfast?' asked Sam to which Gilo responded in the affirmative.

When all first, second breakfasts and drinks had been consumed, we set off in convoy to Rumbledown Farm, the home of Gordon Blackwell, a picturesque farmstead nestled in the rolling hills, about five pleasant miles from the centre of Buntingford Smedley.

After 15 minutes of driving, punctuated by a stop for Biffa to relieve himself in a bush, disquieting a resting stray cat, we reached the outer gates.

We got out of our cars and morphed into amateur Inspector Morses with Flash dropping down onto one knee, inspecting the ground, rubbing it a bit, rubbing his chin and rubbing it again to remove the mud.

'I declare that a vehicle, size unknown, has recently left the farm as the tyre marks are still fresh on the ground.'

'What utter bollocks, don't talk out of your arse Flash' replied an amused Jez 'Posh Spice' Dunstan, who unclipped the latch on the gate to enable the convoy of cars to drive slowly to the front of the house.

'Moooooo' came the greeting from one of the residents.

'Cows' said an enlightened Gobshite, only to be met with a cuff around the head from Bread with an accompanying 'thanks Farmer Palmer.'

But this noise had given us hope, and we stealthily rounded the corner hoping to meet Blacky mid-a-milking but instead were met with a small herd of the animals that had been previously identified.

'Udders look empty to me,' said Gilo who actually was a farmer and therefore enjoyed an elevated position within the group.
This insight was accepted with nodding silence and I, having established that the first port of call was to be Rumbledown Farm, was pleased that I had ensured that Gilo had been awake and was still going to join them. We had found him with Biffa, both mid-second breakfasts in The Scone and looking slightly the worse for wear. This was unfortunately confirmed by various emissions and unnatural noises that accompanied our journey to the farm.

'Aren't you an arable farmer?' asked Sam.

'I am that.'

'So how do you know that they've been milked then?'

'Sam, I may be an arable farmer, but I am a man of the soil, of the country,' he grandstanded, 'and so I know when a chuffing cow has been milked and that a bloke like you, what works behind a desk would know nothing about such country matters.'

So having confirmed that the cows had indeed been milked, it also confirmed that Gordon had been there, or at least someone who knew about cows had and that a full search of the property would be appropriate to see if he was still on location.

'Has he got a dog?' asked Gobshite, 'I don't like 'em, I was bitten by my aunt's Pekinese once, vicious little bugger, it bloody hurt,' and he bent down and rubbed his ankle to support his assertion.
'Well, if he has got one it's bloody quiet,' suggested Winners and with the lack of dog established, we started our surveillance of the farmstead by wandering around the perimeter, looking through windows and trying the door handles, all to no avail.

Gordon Blackwell had left the building, well farm, and we decided to extend our search to the neighbouring villages.

A further investigation of the local watering holes, all of which were now open, resulted in a distinct lack of Blackwells and a reduced number of searchers as each pub had its own charms, luring a member or members of the search party into its convivial interior.

The confident convoy that had left The Sacred Scone at 10am now returned as a jaded jalopy of one containing myself and Jez 'Posh Spice' Dunstan, who had asked to be dropped off at The Sacred Scone as he was hungry, leaving me to drive solemnly to 42 Kingston Drive and into the loving arms of my family.

I turned the key in the lock and mustered up enough enthusiasm for a cheery hello, to be greeted by silence for the second time in 24 hours and a note stuck on the fridge.

'Gone to see my mum, lunch is in the oven, hope the Miss Marple bit went well. Love J xx'.'

And with that I slumped into my favourite chair, put the TV on, and started polishing my bat.

I must have dropped off, for I was startled back into action by Jane and the brood reappearing sometime later in the afternoon, full of stories of Nanny and Gramps' pet spaniel and the poo stains on their new carpet. Ella's enquiry as to where the sun didn't shine and why Gramps wanted to put a broom up it elicited a response from Josh that was soon truncated by his mother calling them for a bath. I was silently pleased that he had missed that little trip and started jotting down my team for next week's home match v Kingly Down.

Jane returned with a gang of freshly bathed offspring and poured herself a large and well-deserved glass of wine.
'Any danger of you actually spending any time with your children? she asked.

I nearly ventured that I was just finalising my team for Saturday, but a combination of one of Jane's looks and a sixth sense stopped me in my tracks.

'Nothing would please me more, my little Rottweiler.'

And with that, I took gathered the troops and started to tell them the story of the day, again. Having put them to bed, I poured myself a drink and settled down on the sofa next to Jane and promptly fell asleep.

I made my way to the office on Monday morning, asked everyone, with the regulation script, about their weekends and sat down at my desk to read, with some trepidation, the online edition of The Buttpill, the local rag. The front page consisted of a report of a month-long traffic diversion in the town centre and a story of suspicious nocturnal agricultural activities in the potting shed of 12 Shingledown Road.

'At least we are not on the front page,' I thought, 'maybe we will be hidden in the sports pages.'

I scrolled down to the next page and my false sense of bonhomie was quickly destroyed.
'A stinker of an affair at Bishop's Tackle' screamed the headline, with the unnecessary sub-heading of 'Mass brawl on pitch brings cricket into disrepute.'

I had to admit that it was a very accurate report and had featured quotes from Chris Dingle and a few of the BT players, the Pritchards and oddly from Darren Perkins. Confused as to what someone who wasn't there could add, I then read that Darren was of the opinion that I was 'a poor leader and less of a tactician.' Apparently, it had come as no surprise to Darren that I couldn't dislodge the ball from the cheese, given my inability to hit the thing during a match either.

I couldn't believe what I had just read. A wanton attack on my character, my dexterity and importantly, my cricketing prowess.

'Unbelievable, they didn't even ask us what we thought,' I whined, and threw my pen across the desk before slumping back into my chair. I didn't have much time to sulk before my mobile flashed up the name 'The Badger' and I knew that my morning was about to get much, much worse.

I had contemplated ignoring the vibrations of an irate chair, but instead I answered with a pitiful 'hello Ba.. Badg, umm alright?' Bad ending.

'ALRIGHT, ALRIGHT have you read the bloody report in the newspaper?

'Yes, Badg, and I can't believe they got a quote from Darren Perkins of all people. He wasn't even there.'

'Sod that berk, we are a laughing stock within the whole local and wider cricket community. I won't be able to hold my head up at Wednesday's parish council meeting. You know that Major Foxton-Bossington thinks that Bishop's Tackle and Buntingford should merge, and our ground be sold to property developers as it is.'

'Ahh so that's his agenda,' I thought and tried to placate him with 'it will pass Badg, I mean it's not like we killed anyone did we?'

'Oh for Pete's sake Barry,' he spluttered,

harrumphed a few times and put the phone down.

Maybe I was on tenterhooks on Tuesday, but every corner seemed to carry a sense of cheese. I was sure that I saw a dozen people hold their noses as I waited for my coffee in The Sacred Scone, that one of my design team was being sarcastic when she asked me whether I wanted a cheese and pickle sandwich for lunch and that today was certainly not the day for Delia's Deli to put a local cheddar on special offer, especially advertising that it had a powerful punch. But nothing was to prepare me for the selection meeting that took place that evening.

When I reached The Wreck, I noted that the cars of The Badger, Noodle, and the treasurer were all present. I took a deep breath, remembered that TED Talk and strode head held high through the front door - to be greeted with Edam cheeses strung out across the bar like Dutch hallowe'en decorations and a beaming Badger looking like the devil incarnate.

'Haha funny eh Baz. My idea I thought we should put the whole Edam business to bed. Haha Edam business, not damned business, hahah,' he carried on in a slightly deranged voice.

Noodle just stood there, shaking his head and so I looked for a voice of reason and fixated on Hawk, who simply shrugged his shoulders, suggesting that he too had no idea what had just happened.

'Well enough of that, The Badger continued, 'we gouda get on' and promptly doubled over in a fit of self-induced laughter.

Noodle reluctantly joined in, if somewhat less enthusiastically than his brother, whilst the club treasurer just shook her head and wished she hadn't agreed to attend.
With some calm restored, The Badger sat down, still chuckling to himself, and called the selection meeting to order.

'So Rocky, I mean Barry, so sorry, slip of the old tongue, what's your team for Saturday?'

'The same nine players from last Saturday,' I started before Noodle interrupted me.

'The same nine disgraces you mean.'

'Now, now,' soothed his brother, 'Barry has been told how the club expects his players to Briehave.' He slapped his thigh with some vigour in celebration of yet another cheese-related pun.

The rest of us groaned in support, secretly hoping that he would now stop and that we could continue, for we had the thorny business of what players I should take from Hawk to discuss.

We need two of your bowlers mate,' I said with sympathy tinged with a hint of arrogance.

'You can have Whitey,' said Hawk with glee, 'and who else do you want?'
I had consulted with my inner self prior to the selection meeting and knew that they were expecting me to react negatively to having to select Whitey.

'I agree,' I said much to their collective disappointment, 'and also we'll take Les Saunders'

Whilst only 52, he was also considered a WOC and Hawk, already on the back foot after my downplaying of the Whitey situation, conceded my request for the junior WOC and proceeded to take from Noodle, for this is the way of things.

Noodle, whose ability to control his mind was less than most ten-year-olds, harrumphed and moaned when he heard that the youngster who had scored a fifty the previous weekend and a young seam bowler were to be called up to the second team.

'There goes our chances of beating Pollington Hall,' he said positively.

Noodle also knew that he now needed to find two colts to make up his numbers and that he would need to speak with their parents and cajole them into letting them play for the men's team.

'What about young Sunil Sharma, he's the leading U16 wicket taker, I suggested, 'he has some pace and can bat too.'

Noodle's face, already puce in colour, turned whatever the next darkest shade post-puce is, pucer, or pucier maybe, but whatever it was, he was it.

'Bu, bu, bu no no no, that won't do, no no,' he stumbled, 'no he is better off playing where he belongs, with his age group I meant, you know age group, yes....' he trailed off as the rest of us looked on in disbelief.

Even his brother, the Badger, was somewhat lost for words and weighed up filial loyalty with the MCC's latest guides on equality, diversity and inclusivity. After a while, and with the rest of the committee staring at him, he pronounced,

'Um yes Paul, I think you should choose Sanjiv Sharma, it would be good for him to play a level up. See what they are made of, him I mean, not they,

him.'
'Sunil,' said Hawk.

'Sorry?' said The Badger

'Sunil,' I helped, 'the lad is called Sunil not Sanjiv.'

'Ah yes, Sunil' agreed The Badger

'All the bloody same,' muttered Noodle, thinking that it was bad enough that he had to parade the local curry house on their shirts, let alone 'one of them' playing for him. With that, the meeting was brought to a close.

'Fancy a beer? I asked Hawk, and when he agreed, we retired, pints in hand, to the sofa hiding a large hole in the clubhouse wall that had been made by Biffa connecting its plyboard with Gobshite's head a few years previously, to discuss our impending matches.

For me it was a chance to receive some Whitey management tips.

'So mate,' I began, 'how do you deal with Whitey on a Saturday?'

'It generally starts on a Friday to be fair,' he answered somewhat upbeat, 'he generally sends me a message telling me what end he wants to bowl from, what number he wants to bat and that he doesn't want to meet up before and that he, and the family, would make their own way there. Then on Saturday morning, he messages me to remind me and to make sure that I understood how important he was to the chances of a successful outcome. When we get to the ground, he and family are already there, he has got changed into his whites and is practicing bowling in the nets. The opposition, who may not have even arrived and if they have, they are still in their civvies, look on with interest, noting the way he bowls, the pace, the swing etc. He then will shout to ask what took us so long and start to organise a warmup. By the time this is done, the team is knackered, and I want to give the game up. Then the real fun starts.'

I was numb and confused. At least I now knew what was coming, but should I comply with Whitey's wishes and, god forbid that he plays well, what would I do if he stays in the team? I knew that the WOCs were out for the season, but surely a younger player deserved the chance more than someone in their late 30s, well specifically someone like Whitey. Well ok actually Whitey.

My thoughts were interrupted by Hawk saying, 'and then he shouts loudly from the sidelines that I, and I quote, 'I am a twat of the highest order if I lose

the toss, again.'
The rest of Hawk's descriptive rundown of what I could expect this Saturday washed over me as I tried to balance my thoughts, and made up my mind to resort to referencing the SADFUC manifesto to see what tips I could glean.

'Umm useful mate thanks,' I said, not sure it had been of any use at all. We downed the rest of our pints and parted ways, with Tim Kestrel singing 'Beautiful Day' loudly, and me not entirely in agreement.

The rest of my week was as humdrum as always, work dragged on, Jane droned on, but, for the first time, Saturday could take its time in arriving.

Ben, as always, wanted to know what tactics I would employ against the team from Kingly Down.

'Will you bat first dad?'

'Depends on the toss son.'

Will you bat any higher up this week, after all the guy's above you were rubbish last week.'
'Not sure son.'

'Will you have a punch up again?'

'Go to bed son.'

Jane, normally totally ambivalent to my moods noticed that I was somewhat down in the mouth.

'Are you alright Baz, is it to do with that article?

'No,' I replied, 'more to do with Whitey and the chaos he could cause to my plans.'

'Don't you have a manual or something, you wrote it before the season - sad tosser or something?'

'SADFUC,' I said, without any sense of irony.

Jane stifled a laugh.

'Well yes, I have referred to it and there is of course a section on culture and the like, but well there is nothing on how to deal with Whitey as I never thought that I would have to.' I continued oblivious to her tittering.

'Fail to plan, plan to fail,' she advised and with that went back to bedtime supervision.

Saturday came, as only Saturday can, with sun, apprehension and a protein and carb-rich fry up to prepare me for both cricketing redemption and glory.

'Kingly Down is a good side,' I thought, 'they came runners-up to Pillingsbury in the league last year, but today's match is at The Wreck and home advantage would give us a fighting chance. I instantly regretted the last thought.'

Jane had given me a book on mindset and manifestation for Christmas the previous year and it had remained, untouched, on my bed side table since then. However, I had picked it up in the last few days, maybe because of what had happened at Bishop's Tackle, and had briefly read a chapter on something vague, called being present.

I had given it a go during the week, trying to be more present with Jane, the kids and at work and I am not sure that I did that good a job to be honest. I was always preoccupied with Saturday's match and the carnage that Whitey could cause if I let him.

I was therefore a somewhat distant figure at the family breakfast table on Saturday morning. Jane busied herself with placing, and in some cases replacing, plates of food in front of the assembled and we tucked in, with varying degrees of relish. The kids multi-tasked with utensils and iPads, whilst I ate absent mindedly, using my fork to practice various imaginary cricket shots.

'Earth to Barry,' chimed Jane, 'Ben is asking you

something.'

'Eh, what, sorry, yes son what did you say?'

'Dad, can I be the mascot for today's match?' asked the future club captain.

'Sure son, why not,' replied the current club captain, perhaps not entirely consciously or understanding the chaos that it could cause both domestically and at The Wreck.

An overjoyed and triumphant Ben, smirked at his siblings, one of whom didn't care and the other seeking revenge, and asked permission to leave the table as he needed to prepare. The time in the Briggs household was 9:46am and the given time to leave was 12:30.

'Like father, like son,' sighed Jane and focused on dealing with the rising conflict arising between Josh and Ella, the former not wanting to go to the match if Ben was to be the mascot and the latter telling him to not be a baby and that it would be fun to see Ben copying everything that dad did. Jane wasn't sure that this was the advice that her only daughter should be giving to her brother but decided that Ella had a point and that it would be interesting to see how Ben would behave.

I had always hated the time between breakfast and

when we needed to leave. I couldn't settle into anything and was snappy and anxious. I paced up and down the lounge, occasionally looking out of the window to make sure that there wasn't any unforecasted storm looming. When I got in the way of Jane hoovering, yet again, I went to make another cup of tea, my fifth.

'Baz go and polish your bat or something,' said an exasperated wife.

"I did that this morning,' I replied, but decided that I needed to check my kit for the third time today. So, I wandered upstairs and repacked my bag, polished my spare bat and practiced a few shadow shots in the mirror. I looked at my watch and it showed noon exactly and I decided that it was high time that I put on my ill-fitting training gear and, when dressed, I descended the stairs as regally as I could whilst lugging my kit bag, commonly known in cricketing parlance as a coffin, due to its box-like appearance, not because it contains the bodies and souls of dead cricket dreams.

Ben, having been in his room since his appointment as match mascot, also emerged at the top of the stairs at the same time as me.

'We're like two captains coming out of their changing rooms at Lords.'

His appearance created much amusement in his

siblings and concern from his mother. Taking his duties seriously and having seen various international cricket captains do the same, he was dressed in full cricket whites, his school jacket and one of my flat caps to replace the lack of anything suitable.

Jane thought of saying something but decided against it. Josh and especially Ella however were less judicious. After much pointing and laughing, Ella reminded Ben that there was no school on Saturday and that oversized caps from Peaky Blinders definitely did not go with cricket whites and a school blazer. Whilst delivering this Trinnie-esque eulogy she was herself in fact wearing pink leggings, a lime green t-shirt, blue Pegga Pig baseball cap topped off with a witch's hat.

'How do you know what Peaky Blinders is?' asked her mother.

'Uhh, a friend at school is allowed to watch it,' she replied, and before she could be questioned any further, she skipped out to the car.

Ben, however, paid no attention to their jibes and came over to me for an inspection.

'Very smart son,' I said approvingly, pleased at the effort that the future captain had made.

And with that, we piled into the car and set off for another enjoyable day at The Wreck.

Ben had fused his mascot duties with that of a team strategist and had also spent some of the time in his bedroom writing down tactics that he felt that his dad would need to employ against Kingly Down. He pulled out his notebook, an action noted by his siblings who nudged each other, and licked his left forefinger to turn to the page that was headed 'taccctics (sic) for Dad's match v Kingly.'

'Dad, he started, 'I have some ideas for today's match, are you ready?

I wasn't sure if I was, but I also knew that my first-born was about to deliver his thoughts anyway, so I needed to be prepared.

'Ok son, fire away.'

Ben sat in the back of the family SUV, occupying the seat next to the left side window, giving him direct access to the driver, in this case me. To his right sat his brother Josh and his sister Ella, both of whom had turned to look at Ben in anticipation of his latest attempts to become their father.

'Dad, I think that we should tell everyone that they should properly warm up before the match. That's what Miss Simms says to us before PE.'

Josh and Ella couldn't disagree with the opening statement and so stayed quiet, with the latter deciding that if this was the level of conversation, then she would go back to her iPad.

'Ok son,' I answered, also somewhat relieved, before Ben made his second point.

'I heard Miss Simms say to Miss Walters that Uncle Winners was well fit and that then she said that she would like to take his wicket. Does she even play cricket dad?'

I spluttered and nearly drove into the back of the car in front, but any consideration of a response was thwarted by Jane who said, as they passed Ye Olde Millstone, 'isn't that Gordon Blackwell?'

CHAPTER 11 - KINGLY DOWN (H)

I swerved across the road as I simultaneously tried to see whether that was indeed the missing WOC and get my family safely to the ground.

'Jesus Barry,' exclaimed Jane, checking to make sure all the kids were still strapped in.

'Sorry gang,' I replied cheerfully, oblivious to the terror on my children's faces.

'Doesn't he owe the team money after that Cheddar thing,' she asked, moving her mind away from Winner's middle wicket.

'Stilton,' I said, somewhat pedantically, 'but yeh he does, I need to tell the guys. Are you sure that it was Blacky?

'Well, it looked like him,' she said definitively.

I drove on in silence, whilst working out how to incorporate this knowledge into my strategy of overcoming Kingly Down and Jane made a mental note to have a private chat with her first born and find out what else he had learned at school.

As always with a home game, we were the first to arrive at the ground, well technically The Badger was as the bar needed opening and Doug was thirsty, but I was the first of the team to arrive.

'Afternoon Badg, you're looking fighting fit.' I said, instantly regretting using that metaphor, if indeed that is what it was.

'A fine day to get your first win. Make up for last week's fiasco,' he responded unsmilingly

As we parked, I had noticed that the groundsman was pushing the heavy roller up and down the pitch, under the watchful, albeit disinterested, eyes of the early arrivals and Dave the dog. Once he had decided that it was flat enough, he lit another cigarette and started to mark out the playing area with white paint.

We walked to the pavilion, and I went into the changing rooms to carefully deposit my bag in the corner that I always used. I heard gravel crunching under approaching car tyres, signalling the arrival of the rest of my team all wearing their travel uniforms, all except Whitey who thought it was a waste of both time and beer vouchers.

One by one they entered the changing rooms, deposited their bags, amidst a series of 'howdo's', 'how was our week's' and went out to inspect the pitch, which was shimmering under the bright sun.

I noticed this flagrant violation of first team rules by Whitey and made a mental note to bring this up with him later. My thoughts were however interrupted by the sound of a convoy of cars snaking its way up the driveway to the club, signalling the arrival of the Kingly Down team. All local eyes, including Dave the dog, turned to inspect the arrivals as they disembarked, stretched and proceeded to remove their coffins, bags and other assorted paraphernalia from their cars.

As with every club up and down the country, the first thing that the opposition does is to size each other up to try and understand who does what. Opening batters will look at all the tall guys and decide that they are the opening bowlers and try and calculate how quick they will be, whilst the actual bowlers look at the short, stocky guys and wonder how they can hurt them.

I had performed my familial duties, which involved making sure that Jane had satisfactorily laid out the picnic blanket, assorted digital appliances, snacks and children, whilst I started precisely arranging my kit in the changing room. Having established that both family and kit were as I would have wanted, I made my way out of hiding and walked to the middle for a quick chat with the groundsman.

'Morning mate how's she playing today?' I asked, unsure as to why the strip of grass was a female.

'She's a flat un,' he replied, understandably as he had just spent half an hour rolling it, 'so you better win the toss and bat.'

Happy that the flat pitch was matched by a warm early summer sun, I laid out the cones and other training implements, called my troops to arms and gave them a brief update on the pitch and, after a quick mental scan of the SADFUC manifesto, I proceeded to deliver my shower-inspired, pre-match speech aimed at inspiring optimum performance.

I must admit that when I had read the quotations that I was about to release, they sounded quite plausible in my head.

'Lads remember – success is like a good cover dirve, it's all about timing, commitment and looking magnificent while doing it,' I delivered.

Confused silence was interrupted by Gilo.

'Baz, have you been drinking?'

I shook my head, mainly at my stupidity at not practicing that line out loud first and realising how daft it sounded.

So, I went back to the basics of cricketing motivational speeches by telling the batsmen to 'see out the new ball' and the bowlers to 'keep it tight'. When your mind is already discombobulated, you can't help but wonder whether you have already lost your audience. But these more cliched utterances seemed to land well and armed with these insights, the team went through its warm-up, the degrees of intensity depending on whether I was watching or not, everyone mindful of the season-ending injury suffered by Chocks Tillwell.

Whilst this spectacle was taking place, the Kingly Downers were engaging in a gentle stroll around the ground, interspersed by the occasional stretch and were watching us with interest as we jogged between cones and attempted to touch our toes.

I found the Kingly Down captain at the tail end of their rambling committee and invited him to change the direction of his walk towards the middle to perform the customary toss of the coin.

We were barely ten paces into that journey when there was a loud, high pitched, piercing scream from the pavilion. We stopped in our tracks and turned, along with much of the rest of the assembled throng towards the source of this hideous sound and witnessed a blazered blonde boy in full whites and an oversized Peaky Blinders hat sprinting towards the us.

'Wait for me dad,' shouted Ben, 'you said I could be mascot remember.'

'Ah yes, my son, Ben,' I mumbled, 'I said that he could be the mascot for today's match. He's keen you see.'

Ben sprinted and came to stand proudly alongside me and declared that we could proceed. A bemused KD captain looked at father and son, started to say something, decided against it and looked stoically straight ahead.

Once we reached the middle, Ben stuck his hand out.

'Could I please ask the home captain to pass me the official coin,' he said in a voice that I had never heard him use before.

Ben had once seen a mascot toss the coin on TV and wasn't going to miss this opportunity. He took it from me and proceeded to turn it over, inspecting its authenticity.

I was secretly proud when he told both of us what was expected of them and sagely tossed the coin up into the air.

'Heads,' came the call and we followed the tumbling coin as it landed on the hallowed turf, her Majesty the Queen staring back at us.

Ben, disappointed for his dad, considered calling it a false toss, but decided that this wouldn't be correct and instead asked the winning captain of his decision.

I shook hands with their captain and with Ben, which seemed a little strange from my point of view, and started to walk back towards the pavilion ready to signal what our teams would be doing for the next couple of hours.

I flicked my index and middle fingers up and down rapidly, imagine the rabbit you made shadows from as a kid, then imagine that this rabbit was headbanging, well you may get the picture, but anyway this was the accepted signal to indicate that we were bowling first.

Whilst the Bishop's Tackle brethren, especially their bowlers, looked suitably happy, my rabbit flicking fingers were met with the opposite reaction from my troops.

'Not even having your son toss the coin makes a

difference,' said Whitey morosely.

Talking of the non-effective mascot, Ben had spent the walk back excitedly providing me with the tactical advice that he had written in his notebook, which was based upon his captaincy of last year's U12 side and supplemented by the two minutes he had just spent in the middle.

'Open with Uncle Bread and Whitey, dad,' he ventured, 'they are both well quick and I don't think that the oppo will like them.'

'Thanks son, I will think about it,' knowing full well that I would open with Bread and Leslie Saunders, in a straight WOC for WOC swap.

Ben had continued to venture his opinions on what I should do whilst fielding, mainly based on what he would have done and how he would have marshalled his team to inevitable glory. One piece of advice stopped me in my tracks and caused me to look curiously at my son.

'Luke stands up to Aaron, he said, adding 'it was my idea.'

If you are not au fait with the term 'standing up,' let me enlighten you. It's a term used when the wicket keeper abandons his normal position of being 10-15 metres behind the stumps when a medium-to-quick bowler is in action and stands right behind them instead. You may rightly question why this would be done, given the chances of getting one in the mush is a lot greater. The main reasons are to kid the batter into thinking that the 'keeper is good, that the bowler isn't that quick, to stop the batter advancing outside of their allotted areas and to have a greater chance of providing some advice on their technique, how to improve their looks and question the validity of their parentage.

I thought about this with our wicket-keeper, Gobshite, in mind and wondered if he had the skills to stand up to any of our faster bowlers but, maybe more importantly, I marvelled at Ben's tactical nouse and considered whether, even though he was just 12, I could utilise these rare skills as part of our pre-match planning.

'I'll have a think son,' I replied, 'good idea though.'

Ben beamed with pride and puffed his chest out as he strode confidently towards the pavilion, ready to tell his mother and siblings of his major contribution to their dad's sporting success.

Whilst he was boring his family and others stiff, we had assembled on the side, replete in our Taj Mahal Indian restaurant sponsored shirts, for our first home game of the season. The massed throng of our fans, all twenty of them, including Mohammed Ibrahim, the proprietor himself, were scattered about the benched area outside of the pavilion, muttering encouragement.

'Go well.'

'All the best and remember no fighting.'

We stepped over the white line onto the field of play and proceeded to jog and stroll our way to the middle. I had been deep in thought since we had lost the toss as I still needed to inform our team who the opening bowlers would be. If you remember, The Badger had banned Blacky and so

Bread needed a new opening bowling partner.

As if to remind me as to what my decision ought to be, Whitey was twirling his bowling arm around vigorously and randomly bursting into sprints, as he would have done if he was bowling in a match.

'Bread, you start at the Belltower End, and Les, can you start from the pavilion please,' I instructed, ignoring the texted instructions that I had received from Whitey last night and again this morning on which end the sender should open the bowling from and, if the team was batting first, where he should bat.

'Oh my god Bazza' exclaimed the irate Whitey, 'I open the bowling for the seconds and Les 'ere, don't.'

'In the first team,' I replied, stressing the level at which Whitey was now playing, 'we open with a quick, Bread, and normally Blacky, but given he is banned, we are going for a like for like with Les,' feeling that I needed to explain myself.

'That's rubbish,' came the retort, 'you should open with your best bowlers, and that includes me.'

I was about to answer, when Gilo stepped forward and towered over the upstart. 'Whitey,' he said menacingly, 'even though Baz is a bit annoying, a cricket saddo and has nothing else going on in his life, he is the captain of this side and therefore we do as he says. Understand?'

Whitey was about to protest, when Gilo took another step forward and The Badger, who doubled up as the home umpire, suddenly appeared and suggested that I needed to take charge of my team and start the match and not another brawl.

More terrified of Gilo's intentions than The Badger's intervention, Whitey backed down and, with hands firmly in pockets, skulked off to stand at his allotted fielding position.

Whilst my authority was being tested, the Kingly Down batters had walked out to the middle and were leaning on their bats watching Whitey's petulance. But now that I had regaled control, thanks to Gilo, they separated and walked to their respective ends.

Cricket grounds have two ends, even though it is round, and these ends usually have names, one of which is generally the Pavilion End, as this is the edifice that forms its backdrop. The other is normally somewhat shorn of in-ground landmarks and must rely on something else for its naming protocol.

In the case of The Wreck at Buntingford Smedley, we have the Belltower End, so called because there stands the only remnant of a medieval manor that served as the generational family home of the main lords of the manor the Cholmondley-Smythes. The Wreck, along with most of Buntingford Smedley and its surrounds, was once part of its estate and legend has it that Sir Horace Cholmondley-Smythe had to forfeit the land to pay off a gamblingdebt

owed to Egbert Fitznibble, the 4th Earl of Plumbleigh, who was coincidentally a member of the MCC. To ingratiate himself with that venerable institution, he bequeathed it to the local cricket team and, whilst no Fitznibble or Cholmondley-Smythe has played for the club in years, their legacy towers over the ground in the shape of the aforementioned structure.

With history and scandal as his backdrop, Ian 'Bread' Daly moved Sam exactly three steps to increase his chances of stopping the ball and satisfied with his repositioning, he started his sprint towards the crease.

The match proceeded in a reasonably processional fashion, the bowlers keeping things tight, as instructed pre-match, and the batters running the occasional single and dealing mainly in fours. After the initial ten overs, the score was 56-0 and I mentally reached into the SADFUC dossier and sought out the chapter on affecting change. And it didn't matter how or where I looked, one part of this strategy had to involve the use of Dave 'Whitey' White.

Winners had replaced his mate and business partner Bread Daly, and reluctantly I looked around to Whitey, who had been trying to get my attention for the last twenty minutes through a series of motions indicating that he was ready to step into the battle. These included whirling his bowling arm, left in his case, vigorously in a circular fashion and loudly declaring it warm, running a few steps and miming his full bowling action without the ball and, when he received it as part of the routine of returning it from the wicket keeper to the bowler, he would rub it strenuously on his trousers to polish one side and only when he was happy would he throw it back to the bowler, who had been waiting, double-teapot for a few minutes.

Taking care of the ball, unlike Jez Dunstan's actions in the previous match, is a sacred part of cricket. Some teams have a dedicated ball polisher, whose job it is to impart maximum amount of shine on one side of the ball and keep the other side scuffed. You may ask why? I don't really know, but I can tell you that it is the fault of science, physics specifically I believe, for when one side is shiny the ball curves through the air as opposed to going in a straight line, thus foxing the batters.

Reluctantly, I passed the ball to Whitey who started five minutes of meticulous field setting, where each player was positioned on an exact blade of grass and ordered not to move from it. Whilst this performance was taking place, the batters were indulging in a loud, mid-pitch chinwag which consisted of a discussion on what they supposed the mid-innings tea would be like.

'I hope there is not too much cheese,' said one.

'I like Stilton, but I heard there was a shortage in the village in the last week.'

'Yes, I heard that but let's hope that I don't need to fight you over what little there is.'

Ignoring our scowls and sarcastic laughter, they walked back to their respective ends and as Field Marshall White had completed his undertaking, umpire Badger lowered his arm to signal that the game may continue. At this Whitey came hurtling in, bowled a straight ball and watched as it sailed back over his head into the car park.

'No fielder there, Whitey,' chortled Gilo, to the amusement of the Kingly Down team and annoyance of his bowler, who stormed back to his mark and awaited the safe return of the ball. However, this wasn't a straightforward exercise as it had rolled under one of the parked cars and needed the intervention of Ben the Mascot to retrieve it. The eager prodigal son, having successfully salvaged the ball, scrambled back up, turned around and threw it back to the nearest fielder, who happened to be me, and I wasn't prepared for what he looked like.

'You'd better go see your mother to get cleaned up,' I said, eager not be involved in any domestic derailing of my attempts to wrest victory.

Ben looked down at his cricket whites, which were anything but, and ran back to his mother.

'Ben-ja-min, she cried, 'look at the state of you, you're covered, absolutely covered in oil.'

Ella and Josh however looked on with wide grins on their faces as they bathed in the glory of seeing their eldest brother squirm. He too was aghast, not necessarily due to the addition to his mother's workload, but because his U13s side was playing Pillingsbury tomorrow and he only had one set of playing whites.

'You can't stay in those clothes,' she said, 'you'll need to get changed into something else.'

'But I don't have any spare clothes,' he whined.

And so it came to pass that the proud mascot, former captain of the Buntingford Smedley U12s, once wearing pristine whites, his school blazer and an oversized Peaky Blinders hat was left to sulkily sit beside his gleeful siblings wearing just his dad's oversized training top with the overly long arms as an ill-fitting smock.

I had heard some of the kerfuffle but was trying to focus on keeping my bowling attack on the straight and narrow. The batters were laying into them, and the score was now 101-0 after 15 overs, with Dave White's bowling figures and ego suffering the most. Things did not improve much for the rest of the Kingly Down innings, for as much as I shuffled my bowlers around, they continued to smite them all over The Wreck until Les the WOC was brought back on to restore some order by using WOCery to elicit an error and make the all-important breakthrough. We wearily trotted over to Les and congratulated him, all except Whitey who was too busy sulking at the unfair treatment that he had received, as I had unceremoniously removed him from the bowling attack after just three overs.

However, if we thought that this would be the start of a change in our fortunes, we were wrong as the next batter continued where the last one had left off and swatted our assortment of bowlers all round The Wreck and when the 40th over had been bowled, we all trooped off for tea with Kingly Down having scored 240-1.

I had previously told you that the mid-innings tea is the highlight, for some, of the whole afternoon's experience and I am proud to say that the Buntingford Smedley offer is ranked highly in the non-existent league table of local teas.

Tradition had it that the first team captain's wife, Jane in my case, would make the first home tea of the season, but Whitey had called me in the week insisting that his wife make this pivotal tea as part of a thank you for being selected in the first team.

Lorraine White had driven into the car park, family in tow, during the Kingly Down innings and proceeded to transport Tupperwares, baskets and paper plates wrapped in foil from the car to the pavilion. Numerous pairs of eyes followed these multiple journeys wondering what culinary treasures she could be carrying, what the quality of said goods would be like and, in Jane's case, a mild panic as to whether our tea would remain in top spot after its unveiling.

The Kingly Down opening batter had his bat held high to celebrate the 95 runs he had scored in their total and was greeted with both applause and ridicule from his teammates, enthusiastically accusing him of 'jug avoidance.' I had led my team's half-hearted applause for the opposition and patted my weary fielders on the back as they shuffled listlessly towards the sanctuary of our changing room. I felt that an invigorating pep talk was needed to rally our beleaguered troops and, as I faced the wall, one foot on the bench to remove my boots I started to deliver a soliloquy.

'Lads, hard work out there today, flat pitch and well, we bowled bad lengths didn't we. But it's the same pitch for both sides, we need to dig in and bat long, don't we?'

'Don't we?' I repeated when my first salvo was greeted by silence.

More silence. I turned round to realise that I had been addressing an empty changing room.

I shook my head at the lack of respect for my authority and made a note to update that section of the SADFUC document. I put on my Crocs and, still muttering to myself, I went to see what Lorraine White had produced in the way of a tea.

Upon entering the bar-cum-tearoom I was greeted by the odd sight of both teams and assorted hangers-on forming a cordon about two feet off the edge of the table, unsure as to what they should do. I looked for Jane, in the way of an explanation but, upon our eyes meeting, she turned away, her shoulders heaving up and down in an ill-disguised attempt to hide her uncontrolled laughter.

I realised that she would be of no use and wondered what she was finding so funny, I was aided in deducing this when I heard a sobbing Lorraine, eyes puffy, nose red and shiny, who was saying to no one and everyone, 'it ain't my fault, I picked up the wrong bag ditn't I.' Her husband, and chief advocate, was standing next to her looking sheepish, not sure whether he should comfort her or not. He started to add to her statement of guilt but decided against it and instead performed like a hungry goldfish.

The sea of players and hangers-on had parted as I progressed towards the pool-cum-tea table to be greeted by a luminous riot of sugar, headed by a green Colin the Caterpillar cake sitting somewhat proudly on a pink, plastic cakestand.

'It's our Carlee's berfday party later and I picked up

'er bag.' she offered up as the reason why the teams and hangers-on would be faced with eating poor Colin, jam sandwiches, French Fancies and Haribos.

'Well, this is umm, interesting,' I tried, whilst shaking my head, 'we don't have much choice, so let's get on with it.'

And with that, I picked up the cake knife and was about to dissect the innocent Colin, only to be stopped by a sticky, grubby hand attached to a sticky, grubby Carlee White.

'Ere watcha doing to my party tea,' she asked indignantly.

'Umm well we are having our cricket tea, Carlee,' I explained.

'Well that's not your cricket tea, it's my berfday party tea' she said, not unreasonably.

I stood and observed the youngest of the White clan, who in turn had her arms crossed and was staring back at me expecting an explanation as to why I was attempting to steal her birthday fare.

Before I could provide her with the required explanation she continued 'it's not for you, it's for my friends who is coming for my berfday party.'

'Yes, but that's later, and it's at your house,' I tried soothingly.

'No, it's 'ere 'cos my food's 'ere,' she replied.

Thankfully at this stage, Lorraine had regained a modicum of composure and came over to put the facts of the matter to her adamant daughter. She took Carlee by the arm and led her away and explained that her birthday tea was to include tuna sandwiches and quiche. A loud boo emanated from the folks gathered around the table as a gallant Whitey cleared several of them out of the way and carefully picked up Colin the Caterpillar and took him, gratefully, back to his box.

Colin's eviction sparked a free for all as the hungry cricketers, umpire, kids, wives and general malingerers went hell for leather on what remaining goodies remained on the table. Apart from the interesting menu, the other notable difference between your run-of-the-mill cricket tea and a five-year old's party is the quantity, a difference that is starkly highlighted when you have a man such as Gilo in your team. The 120kg opening batter picked up a plate and threw a large paw at the various sugary treats and walked away with a vast pile of sustenance, leaving the rest to fight over what was left.

'I'll pop down to the shops Baz and get some proper food,' said Jane, grasping the magnitude of the problem.

I sighed and went back to the changing rooms to see how I could get my still hungry team to focus on winning a match that seemed beyond us.

'Good tea that,' announced Gilo as we belched his way into the changing room.

'It wasn't, was it Gilo,' contended Gobshite, 'I had a bloody jam sandwich and a lump of sticky Haribos. I'm blooming starving.'

'Jane's gone to get some sandwiches, you can have some whilst you are waiting to bat.'

235

Gobshite muttered something about biting the head of Colin the bleeding Caterpillar, to which Whitey was about to respond when he realised that his position in the affair was weak.

With team harmony at an all-time low and my SADFUC document in tatters, we walked back onto the pitch to recommence hostilities.

Half an hour later, with the match in full swing and our batting in early trouble, I saw Jane pull into the car park, remove some bags and run feverishly towards me.

'I just saw Gordon again.'

CHAPTER 12 - THE BETRAYAL

The match had come to a swift conclusion, as the Kingly Down bowlers made short work of our batting line up and we lost the match by 100 runs. We felt that we may have had a chance of an unlikely victory when Winners and Gobshite were sharing a stand of 65 which, at one point, had instilled in us a false sense of confidence, only for reality to set in when the latter danced down the pitch, dreaming of glory, missed the ball entirely and walked back to the pavilion to be met with shakes of heads and mutterings.

The Kingly Down team, disheartened by our poor efforts and the tea debacle, had left The Wreck quite quickly after the match had finished and I really should have assembled my disheartened team in the changing rooms and delivered a post-match-mortem. But my mind was on other things, namely, how could we find and apprehend Blacky, get the money back and start the process of reintegrating the devious WOC into the team, to stave off the very real threat of relegation to the league below.

After everyone had showered, changed and assembled in the bar-cum-tearoom, I tapped a spoon against my pint glass to call the masses to attention.

'Lads, Jane saw Blacky twice today, the second time was when she went to get the replacement tea after the Caterpillar cake incident. He clearly thinks that we have forgotten about the money and is starting to get more confident and spend more time in the village.'

A murmur of assent rippled through the room as the assembled waited, with bated breath, for me to outline my cunning strategy for capturing the WOC and recovering their money.

'I think we strike whilst the iron is hot,' I continued, 'so I suggest we all assemble tomorrow morning and start Operation Capture Blackwell.'

I proceeded to outline what I loosely had labelled a plan, but as the SADFUC document contained exactly no information on how to apprehend errant non-debt paying G. Blackwells, I was reduced to making it up on the fly.

'OK lads, I suggest that we go to different places in the village from 11am tomorrow to spread the proverbial net, as it were. Blacky is bound to go to one of his usual haunts and we can nab him there.'

'Ow we gonna lift 'im skip?' Gobshite asked, the very question that I hadn't wanted anyone to ask as I hadn't actually thought of a method to apprehend Blacky.

'Well,' I started, 'I think that whoever finds him

should perform a citizen's arrest and call for the rest of us to come to his aid.'

'Rubbish,' exclaimed an animated Gilo, 'whoever finds him should give him a walloping and sit on 'im until the rest of yoos come.'

The room was split over the two suggestions, with the relative size and bravado of the punter being the criteria for which camp one placed oneself in. With most of the team not being the size of Gilo, and not wanting to have public dust up, my suggested course of action was adopted, leaving me with the task of researching how one performed a citizen's arrest.

Having agreed upon the method of obstructing the supposed villain, the next job for our self-proclaimed group of vigilantes was to decide who would be positioned where. This conversation lasted considerably longer than the methodology chat as there were some prime locations to be allocated and certain members of the group were adamant about where they would be positioned.

'The Prickly Oyster for me,' said Gilo steadfastly, adding unhelpfully, 'who's joining me there?' Five others put their hands up, meaning that there were six happy to stake out the pub.

'Paul and I will be lunching at Ye Olde Millstone tomorrow anyway, so we will keep an eye out for him there,' said The Badger and, as no one wanted to have lunch with Noodle, they remained at two.

'We've got some work, which we could do at The Sacred Scone,' said Winner, to which Flash and Sam, the Stevens brothers, added 'we'll join you there.'

So, everyone who had been affected by Blacky's actions plus Noodle, had been allocated a place to establish a stakeout. However, there were other places that the fugitive would consider part of his Sunday routine.

'Right lads, that's not going to work, is it? What about his farm, Bob's Bookies, the supermarket etc?

'I'm staying at the Oyster,' said Gilo.

'I'm playing dominos there tomorrow, so I am also in the pub,' said Stan Clarke.

With The Prickly Oyster fully allocated, I needed to make sure that we had every other location covered.

'We're good for The Scone,' said Winners at which Flash suggested that a Sunday curry buffet would be a good idea and Sam agreed.

'You know our plans,' said The Badger.

That just left the bookies, the supermarket and Blacky's farmstead.

'OK Gobshite you go and wait in the supermarket car park,' I said to roars of laughter and cat calls from the others about his dating habits.

'Doug, you take the farm,' I instructed and noticed Dave looking at me, a low growl starting to emit from his mouth. 'You too Dave,' I said, and his tail started wagging with delight.

'Right Jez, that just leaves me and you to lose a few quid in Bob's Bookies.

So with a clear location plan and a vague notion of how this capture would take place, we broke off into smaller groups and scattered across the bar-cum-tearoom.

Les Saunders and Whitey, who had played today, had not been part of the Stilton incident and so had been excluded from these discussions. Les had been somewhat relieved to know that he would not need to explain to his wife that he would be spending his Sunday on some wild goose chase, whereas conversely, Whitey was somewhat put out that his new first team chums would be bonding, albeit in pairs, without him for he was keen to repair relations after his performance on the pitch and the tea debacle.

'Where d'ya want me Baz?' he asked somewhat vaguely, leaving the response open to a great deal of variability. Gilo, in fact, did open his mouth to respond but, very much out of character, decided not to say anything.

'Well Whitey, you weren't there at the match and didn't lose any money to Blacky, so we don't need your services.' I responded diplomatically.

Whitey though also wanted to be out of the house on Sunday to avoid the aftermath of both Carlee's birthday sleepover and any fallout from the tea incident and so tried again.

'I know that Baz, but an extra pair of eyes, ears and hands would be good, yeh?'

I wished, not for the first time, that I had never selected Whitey for the Kingly Down match. He had bowled badly, scored exactly zero runs, his wife had brought the teas of Buntingford Smedley to its knees and here he was, trying to involve himself in Operation Capture Blackwell.'

Gilo was leaning against the bar talking with Biffa, who had wandered in for a cleansing pint before they both headed off to The Prickly Oyster. He decided that his intervention was necessary at this point, and he turned to Whitey.

'Whitey your bowling was shit, your batting was shitter and your tea was the shittest I have ever had. The last thing we now need is you arsing up our watch.'

With that he turned to Biffa and said, 'we're doing an all dayer at the Oyster tomorrow if you fancy it?'

Whitey, steam venting from his ears, slammed his pint down on the table and marched out of the door, plotting how he could destroy the plan that he had heard, but was not a part of.

'I'll get that sweaty farmer back, see if I don't,' he muttered darkly.

Sunday morning in the Briggs household was like any other Sunday apart from today I would not be taking Ben to his U13 match, so not quite the same. I had explained our plan to capture Gordon Blackwell to Jane whilst she was sorting out Ben's oil-free(ish) kit, making the kids' breakfasts and generally tidying up. I was left scratching my head and wondering about the sanity of the female of the species when Jane asked me, using language that would make a porn star blush, whether I thought that recovering £50 was more important than being with my family on Sunday, especially given that I had spent all Saturday playing with my friends.

I didn't really know how to respond to Jane, at this or at any other time, when she gets all unreasonable like that. I mean, what am I supposed to do?

I decided to speak with Ben on how to approach the upcoming Pillsbury fixture instead. Even though he wasn't captain of the U13 he was a senior player, if you know what I mean, because he is my son. I needed to give the sort of pep talk I would give my own team.

'Remember to always concentrate son. Eye on the ball and attack it. Don't go in half-hearted as you will fail,' I advised, 'be positive. All the way Ben, all the way.'

'And remember to have fun,' chipped in Jane.

'Fun comes from winning son,' I added.

'And remember whatever happens we love you,' she said as only a mother can.

I turned around to look lovingly at her, but as soon as she saw me, that soft Jane turned to rock and she gave me another one of those stares and turned on her heels.

I sighed and picked up the car keys, shouted bye to which I got no response from anyone except Ben, opened the car door and got in. I drove the two miles to the village centre and parked in the market square, waiting for my co-conspirator, Jez Dunstan. Whilst I was waiting, I took the time to scan the local environment for any early signs of

Blacky, but also to see who else had parked in the square, the main car park for the village. Every one of the stakeouts apart from Blacky's farm, Ye Olde Millstone and the supermarket were in the market square, making the capture of any suspect easy. I was looking to my right, noting that Gilo had parked his battered van a few spaces away, when there was a tap on the passenger side window.

'Bloody hell, you scared the bejesus out of me,' I said, relieved that the tapper was Jez Dunstan.

'Haha sorry skip just thought I would make sure you were awake. Just saw Bread and Winners going into the Scone and I'm pretty sure that Gilo and Stan are already in the Oyster.'

'OK cool,' I said, 'do you have your stake money? We can't spend hours in Bob's Bookies and not have a flutter or two.' And with that, I opened the glove compartment and withdrew a clear plastic bag of coins that I had saved up in a glass jar in my study.

'You know Bob takes credit cards, don't you?

'Yes, but if I use these coins then it won't seem like I am spending anything, and Jane won't get even madder than she is already.'

As Jez had rightly predicted, Gilo and Stan, plus Biffa who had taken up the call to arms from the previous night, had taken up their position at the bar of The Prickly Oyster. The rest of the guardians of justice were also in position in their allotted spaces, including Doug and Dave the dog who, situated as they were at the gates to Rumbledown Farm, were somewhat surprised to see a car coming up the road towards them. Having watched several police dramas over the years, Doug slid down his seat to obscure his face from the new arrival. Dave the dog was less accustomed to the correct protocol and instead stuck his head out of the window and barked at the approaching vehicle.

The car stopped at the gates and the occupant got out and walked over to stroke Dave.

'Awight Dougie watcha doin' 'ere?'

'Er hello Whitey, I could ask you the same question?' replied a now upright Doug.

'Nuffink special mate, just come to see Blacky – aint seen 'im for ages 'ave I? You wanna see 'im too?'

'Uhh yeh, same' stuttered Doug, 'gate's locked, I don't have his number, so was waiting to see if he was in or not.'

'I'll call 'im now,' said Whitey and, after scrolling through his contacts, put his mobile phone up to his ear. 'It's ringing,' he said unnecessarily.

Back at the Bob the Bookies, Jez and I had walked tentatively into the shop and were standing by the door, taking in the scene. He had been in a few bookies in his time, mainly for the FA Cup Final and the Grand National horse race, but I was a novice and had never actually been in a bookmaker's shop before.

I looked curiously at the various pages of the Racing Post stuck to the walls under signs proclaiming the names of the places, which I assumed correctly, were the racecourses and wondered what Jane would make of this novel attempt at interior design. Just to the left of these was a row of two fruit machines replete with plastic stools. A small coffee machine and thin cups made up the amenities available to the punters, who currently numbered three – me, Jez and an old man who was at the small window giving the cashier a piece of paper upon which he had scrawled the name of the greyhound that would provide him enough to pop over to the Oyster for a pint of best bitter.

Gilo, Stan and Biffa had been joined at the pub by Gobshite, who had abandoned, after 30 minutes of vigilance, both his companion and his position in the supermarket car park, citing boredom as the key reason for this dereliction of duty.

'The shoppers probably thought you were a perv, hanging about in car parks,' observed Gilo to a reddened Gobbers, who adjusted his crotch and responded with a weak 'you'd know.'

But with that, the supermarket car park position was deemed closed.

At The Sacred Scone, Winners and Bread were engrossed in the contents of their laptops and nursing a couple of flat whites.

'I suppose we ought occasionally to look up and make sure Blacky hasn't slipped in for a chai latte,' suggested Winners.

'The chances of him coming in here are like Whitey's score yesterday mate. Zero. Greasy spoon yes, Sacred Scone no.'

The Stevens brothers had been allocated Sunday lunch at the Taj Mahal Indian restaurant. They dutifully turned up at 11am to see a sign on the door proclaiming that the restaurant was open Monday to Saturday, 12 noon to 11pm.

'I thought Barry, with all his planning, would have checked to see if it was even open on a Sunday,' said Flash, 'but anyway I am bloody hungry, where shall we get some lunch?'

'The Oyster does a good roast,' said Sam, and with that, the two brothers crossed the square to the pub where they were soon standing at the bar with Gilo, Stan, Gobshite and Biffa.

The Taj Mahal Indian restaurant post, having not even opened, was now closed.

Whitey, in the meantime, had tried Blacky a couple of times but the errant WOC hadn't picked up. 'E's either already sozzled or 'is drivin',' noted Whitey, not realising that at that very moment Gordon Blackwell was looking at his phone.

'Bloody Whitey keeps calling me, wonder what he wants?'

The Badger and Noodle spent every Sunday at Ye Old Millstone with their wives and friends from the bowling club and so it was no coincidence that this was their post for Operation Capture Blackwell. What they had failed to tell anyone, including and most importantly me, was that Mrs Blackwell was a member of the bowling club, and she too was a regular attendee of the Sunday luncheon. So, whilst the rest of the Buntingford Smedley team were in the process of abandoning various posts and families to centralise their search for Blacky in The Prickly Oyster, the fugitive was in fact colluding with the club chair and his brother at a rival public house.

'I'll try 'im once more,' said Whitey and proceeded to press the call button on his phone.

'Why are you really here?' asked Doug, to which Dave the dog cocked his head to one side and trained his good eye on Whitey, urging him to respond to his master.

Another call had returned unanswered.

'Truth be known Dougie, I was going to warn Blacky about the money and that he had better return it to the lads. I thought that if I did that then Bazza would keep me in the first team.'

Dave the dog deemed this to be a satisfactory response and turned his head to his master to see whether he agreed. Doug didn't really know what to make of this sudden burst of honesty from Whitey.

'Uhh right, um ok, fancy a pint then?'

'Yeh go on, cheers Doug.'

And with that the siege of Rumbledown Farm also ended, without really starting.

Jez had decided to adopt a strategy of less is more to while away the time at Bob's Bookies. He made a big show of studying the form of the 11:36 bag at Walthamstow, where six pacy greyhounds foolhardily chase a mechanical hare around a circuit, bereft of the knowledge that the result may have already been predetermined. Having selected Crafty Cockney based on both its name and physique, he wandered over to Brenda, Bob's wife who acted as the cashier, and placed £5 each way.

He held his betting slip close to his heart and looked up at the screen to watch the action unfold.

I, on the other hand, had adopted the reverse strategy of many small each way bets, all paid for by the bag of coins that I had taken from my glove compartment which, upon a careful count, had totalled £21.50. I had given it some thought, albeit briefly, before I had left the house that morning and had decided that I would place a £1 each way bet every 30 minutes, in which way my vigil could last the entire day if needed.

I was standing studying the Racing Post wallpaper, not really understanding what all those numbers meant when I saw a likely looking candidate.

'There's a horse running called Barry's Boy'

'Dog,' said Jez.

'How do you know, it could be ok?' I replied. Confused.

'No you idiot, Barry's Boy is a dog, it's in the same race that I have bet on.'

Feeling a bit of a dunce, I walked up to Brenda and asked to put £1 on Barry's Boy, to which she asked for my ticket. I must have been standing there like a small boy lost on his first day at school, as she took pity on me and showed me how to fill in a booking chit. She smiled a sad smile, took my money and gave me back the pink slip to confirm my entry.

The dogs went into their starting traps, Crafty Cockney in trap 6 wearing a pink jacket and Barry's Boy next to him in trap 5 wearing a jaunty jacket of red stars on a black background. The starter waved his flag, the bell rang, the mechanical hare shot out of its hutch and the greyhounds commenced their fruitless chase.

Whilst this was going on, the bar at The Prickly Oyster was extremely busy with various people from the village including the Pritchard's of cheese fame, Chris Dingle and Graham Singleton from the Bishop's Tackle team, Biffa, Gilo, Gobshite, Stan Clarke, the Stevens brothers, who had eaten their roast, and now Winners and Bread, who had completed their work and decided that as Blacky was very unlikely to show his face, they would close The Sacred Scone look out post.

The talk was of the cricket results the day before, with the Dingle gleefully telling the Buntingford Smedley ensemble that they had beaten Chimping Tillbury quite comfortably and that Paul Pritchard had scored a fine century. This brought the conversation back around to the Stilton incident and that, in fact, they were all in the pub because they were all on the lookout for Gordon Blackwell with a view to getting their money back.

'Wouldn't you be better spreading out across the village? asked the Dingle sensibly, to which Gilo replied 'we've tried that, but decided that strength in numbers is a better option.

'Where's your skipper? Him what dug the ball out of me cheese?' asked Mr Pritchard senior.

'Bob's Bookies,' said Bread, adding that it was unlikely that he would abandon his position so lightly.

'Don't 'e know that Gordon doesn't like betting

after the incident with Bob and Brenda?'

'We don't know that either,' prompted Winners, to which Ted downed the remnants of his pint, waved the empty glass in the enquirer's direction and cleared his throat ready to relate the story of the missing betting slip.

Back at Bob's Bookies, Jez and I crumpled up our own slips, as we saw our respective selections limp home a way back from the winner, the Duke of Willingham. Jez had a bit of a wait until his next choice, so he declared himself thirsty and hungry and that he would pop over to The Prickly Oyster for a quick one and be back before the 13:04 race. I was now flying solo, strolled back to the wall and looked at what choices I had for the 12:04 at Romford.

Whitey, having agreed to Doug's suggestion of a refreshment, parked alongside his new ally in the car park of Ye Olde Millstone and noted that The Badger and Noodle were there too. He also noticed a dirty, green, old Land Rover Defender parked in the corner. He didn't know whose vehicle it was but had a strange feeling that it may belong to the man he had been trying to call since 11am. And Whitey would be proved to be right, for as he walked into the lounge bar he saw The Badger, Noodle, assorted partners and others joined in conversation with Gordon Blackwell and a lady that Whitey supposed to be his wife.

Doug and Dave the dog walked over to greet the bowling club group, but Whitey hung around by the door unsure as to what to do. When he had formulated the plan to go and find Gordon, he had done so through anger after being slighted by Gilo, but as he calmed down his selfishness came to the fore and he wanted to show his good side, for what it was, to me and remain part of my first team plans. So, whilst the group was greeting Doug and Dave the dog, Whitey stepped out into the car park and called me.

I was standing alone watching the greyhounds competing in the 12:34 race at White City being loaded into their respective traps with number 4 Topspin Googly holding my hopes. The hare started running, the greyhounds followed, and my phone started to vibrate. My first thought was that it was Jane asking whether we had found Gordon and when I was planning to return home. Then I thought it may be someone who had apprehended Blacky and it was this second thought that made me look at my phone and see, with dismay, that it was Whitey.

As Topspin Googly turned the last bend, valiantly trying to remain in first place, I decided to answer my phone.

'Hi Whitey,' I said, not knowing that he had joined the hunt, 'is this about your performance on the pitch yesterday, because I'm a bit tied up, Jane, the kids you know.'

There is one thing that the likes of Dave White know, and that is when they have the moral high ground, the upper hand if you like. And Whitey knew that now.

'Give it a break Bazza, you're in Bob's Bookies losing money, waiting to see if Blacky turns up,' he said, not pulling any punches.

And before I could splutter 'how do you know' Whitey followed up with 'I know where he is, but it's going to cost you.'

I went silent as it was a strange situation. The mission could come to a successful conclusion within the next hour and I could go home £50 the richer, but the source of the information was untrustworthy, and Whitey was extremely manipulative.

'Name your price Whitey,' I said, noting a Ted Talk where the best negotiations started with honesty.

'A guaranteed first team place for the season, I can't be dropped,' retorted Whitey, showing his metaphorical cards.

'Done, ok tell me where he is.'

Whitey's disclosure of Gordon's location and luncheon guests had sent me reeling and even Brenda calling out for me to pick up my winnings, all £5 of them, went unheeded. I stumbled out of Bob's Bookies and called Gilo.

'He's in Ye Olde Millstone,' I said breathlessly, 'can you call Winners, he is in The Scone with Bread and he can call Flash and he can call Gobshite, and he can call Doug.'

''Yeh, I know mate,' retorted the genial farmer, 'we're all in Ye Olde Millstone with The Badger, Noodle, the Dingle, Biffa, the Pritchard's and Blacky. We're all here, the whole team, come up and have a drink.'

And with that I disconnected and sat in silence.

'Baz, Baz, hello? said Gilo to the group, adding 'odd he's cut me off.'

'Let's create a drinks kitty from the money we just got off Blac, I mean Gordon,' suggested Gobshite.

'First good idea you've had,' retorted Gilo and with that that treachery was complete.

I staggered to my car and leaned against it, the warm noon colouring my already red face. It should have been soothing and relaxing, but I was not feeling any of these emotions. Instead, I felt hurt, betrayed even, as the very guys I had held up to be the pinnacle of the Buntingford Smedley Cricket Club had let me down. And to add insult to injury, Whitey was the one who had told me, albeit with a large string attached.

As I opened the car door and sat in the brown leather seat, I considered my options. I could drive up to Ye Olde Millstone, have that drink and ask Blacky for my share of the winnings, or I could go home to the comfort of Jane and the kids. I sighed, fired up the engine and dreamed of the loving chaos of home, a long bath and polishing my bat in readiness for the next fixture against the early league leaders, Lower Nether Wallop-on-the-Wold. And with that, I set off for home.

CHAPTER 13
- THE FAMILY
FUN DAY

The rest of the season had been unremarkable, which wasn't hard given the incidents that had marked the earlier weeks and months. My relationship with the team had remained frosty for several weeks after the Ye Olde Millstone betrayal, but things were slowly getting better, and I hoped that today's family fun day would put a jaunty cap on the head of this troubled season.

I had been instructed by The Badger to reintegrate Blacky, after the latter had not only settled the debt, but had also agreed to supply the former with free milk and eggs for twelve months. Whilst I had been annoyed with the circumstances, I had to admit that Blacky's performances had gone some way to achieving a mid-table level of respectability.

I had spent any given Saturday on some cricket field or other, trying my hardest to cajole a series of increasingly disinterested adults into the sort of performance that credited their club and provided the results that their main, and only sponsor, Mr. Mohammed Ibrahim, the proprietor himself of The Taj Mahal Indian restaurant demanded of them. I remember that there was one notable incident where, after three defeats in a row, he marched into the Tuesday selection meeting with a list of players that he would like to see selected, which included a new name, Kamal Ibrahim, his 12-year-old son, who he had brought to the meeting.

'Kamal, make the cover drive,' he had instructed, which the sheepish boy had executed to stunned silence.

'There you see, what a player my son is,' beamed the proud father.

'Umm yes thank you Ibrahim,' The Badger had said, 'we will consider him, no doubt.'

'We bloody won't' I had muttered under my breath,

But there was one match in the season that had stood out, not for the inclusion of the 12-year Kamal, but for the fact that the opposition was Pillingsbury and Darren 'Dazzler' Perkins.

I don't know if you have ever been to Pillingsbury, but it is a pleasing little hamlet, located about 5 miles from Buntingford Smedley and can be reached both via a straight road built by the Romans and various paths through farmers' fields. This proximity meant that any fixture against them was considered a derby match and so had to be taken extra seriously. It wasn't only cricket, there were many competitions between the villages including a Yard of Ale contest, of which Gilo was the current champion and an odd event involving the threshing of corn from a specified field, whilst wearing a fancy dress costume. I had never competed in either of those, but Gilo and Gobshite were regular attendees.

This grudge, and threshing event, extended back to the days of the Cholmonley-Smythes when the second lord of the maor's teenage daughter ran off with a strapping farmhand from Pillingsbury and was promptly excommunicated from the family and both villages. The irate land owner stripped the poor farmer of his property, including the field now used for the threshing competition and decreed that all Pillingsburians were persona non grata. Whilst this initially meant that they could not enter the village of Buntingford Smedley, it had subsequently turned into various village versus village contests.

We Buntingford Smedlians had seen Darren Perkins' defection to Pillingsbury as the ultimate in local betrayal and this added extra spice to the already tasty affair. I had selected a formidable team for this match, and we had met at The Sacred Scone as usual to begin the short journey across enemy lines to Pillingsbury. In times gone by there would have been pitch-forked youths manning the entry points to either village, but these had been replaced by speed cameras, which frankly were more dangerous.

We had reached Pillingsbury's Henry VII Playing Fields, decamped to the changing rooms and inspected the ground as I had previously described and, devoid of any mascots or other interference, I had walked out to the middle with their captain and tossed the coin. I continued my losing streak, and we were soon fielding under a gloriously hot August sun. Blacky and the rest of the bowlers were very unhappy with me, I remember.

The crowd for this match was always larger than the twenty or so that normally attended our matches as the locals turned out in force and it is generally a rowdy affair. Whilst the game itself had been a damp squib, the presence of Dazzler amongst his former teammates had created a suitable level of conflict.

Their ground, known locally as the H7 is conveniently located next to the audaciously named Richard of York pub, the scene of many village battles over the years, but only similarity to the Battle of Bosworth Field at our match had been the verbal jousting between Dazzler and his former teammates.

'Traitor,' Gobshite had said as soon as he had seen his former teammate.

'Loser,' leaving it to opinion if Dazzler had been talking about his cricket performance or of his life per se.

Gilo had been the one who had introduced Dazzler to me in the first place and so he had been slightly more reserved, but this did not stop the others letting our former bowler know what they thought of him.

The Pillingsbury faithful had turned up at the pub in good time for the match and were well into their work when their team went into bat. As the runs continued to accumulate, so did the empty pint glasses and, given that there were few Buntingfordians in attendance, they decided that an internal fracas was most appropriate, creating a familiar historical backdrop to the on-field action.

It came as no surprise to me that Dazzler would run through our batting line-up without too many problems. Some short-term resistance from Flash, who had been lifted by the tense atmosphere on the pitch and in the pub, and Gobshite, who was in a feisty mood, especially when Dazzler picked up the ball and threw it at him from ten yards away, had given us hope.

Not for the first time this season, an incensed Gobshite had run towards an opposition player with a piece of wood in his hand, this time his bat.

'You do that again, I'll knock your block off,' he had threatened.

Dazzler smiled his assassin's smile,

'Fancy one in the chops instead?'

This last statement had caused a loss of downstairs control and, when Dazzler had removed Gobber's off stump, the resistance was over.

The watching Mohammed Ibrahim, who had special dispensation to visit Pillingsbury as his was the only Indian restaurant in the area, had made some notes on what he had just witnessed.

'Now Barry,' he had started as I was removing my pads after another dismal personal performance with the bat. 'As the main, and only sponsor, of the club, I have made some ideas as to how we can improve for the next season isn't it.'

And even though I hadn't been in the mood for his thoughts or didn't know if I would even be the captain next year, I had spent the next twenty minutes listening to the virtues of Kamal Ibrahim as a boy and cricketer.

We had fallen to a pitiful and heavy defeat, much to the amusement of the pub dwellers and Dazzler, who had taken great delight in pulling a stump out the ground, attaching the Pillingsbury village flag to it and had run joyfully around the ground singing We Are The Champions.

Things could have gotten ugly, but I had corralled my team into their cars and we had driven back to The Wreck with our tails between our legs. This had been the low point, but we soon started to make improvements, namely the return of Blacky, and had finished the season in mid-table complacency

Outside of running my business, the demands of being a losing first team skipper and occasional family duties, my time had been spent on organising the celebrity match and family fun day, which was due to be held on the Saturday after the final round of league matches, i.e. today.

I had had a few months to organise this season-ending bonanza since Tim 'Hawk' Kestrel, head of Operation Top-Up's event sub-committee, had given me the dual task of contacting both the Wandering Has Beens and various purveyors of children's entertainment, incinerated burgers and overpriced tat.

I had successfully palmed off some of the

responsibility of the family fun day to my PA, who had organised the bouncy castle with Bonzo, currently seen inflating what looked like a giant Tower of London in the corner of The Wreck, adjacent to the remains of what had been a children's roundabout until some local kids tried to have a BBQ on it. Alongside that Mary, a friend of Jane's who owned a craft shop just off the market square, was setting up her display of homemade porcelain jugs and, at Jane's request, she had asked some her fellow crafters to join her, and they too were in the midst of displaying their arty wares.

'Looking good so far Mary,' I encouraged, 'good selection of items there.' I had nearly said tat but managed to control myself.

Walking round the ground I saw our main, and only sponsor.

'Hi Ibrahim, that smells great, making me hungry.'

Mohammed Ibrahim had parked his hastily created food truck, which was, in reality, an old ice cream van with the freezers replaced with hot food holders, to the right of the pavilion, between the pitch and the car park.

'It is going to be a tip top day Barry.'

And with that he continued loading mounds of hot samosas, onion bhajis, chicken tikkas and breads into the display cases. I noticed that he had taken the prime spot closest to both the pavilion and the single power source.

'Reserved the best spot innit, because I am Mr. Mohammed Ibrahim the main, and only, sponsor of

Buntingford Smedley CC.'

The Prickly Oyster, who had initially offered to set up a burger van until they were dissuaded by the proprietor himself at a council meeting, had been reduced to manning a barbecue stall. They had been placed on the other side of the craft stalls to ensure that the Taj Mahal food truck took pride of place.

Tim Kestrel, wearing his cricket flannels, training top and a crimson blazer was walking from stall to stall, clipboard in hand, to ensure that all was in order and, when satisfied that it was, he went into the bar-cum-tearoom to ensure that everything was in order.

'All set Badger?' he asked, adding 'vis-à-vis the refreshments.'

'All set Hawk, I can personally vouch for the freshness of both the bitter and the lager. First rate.'

The next person that I bumped into was Winners who had wanted to do the music and be the event emcee, as he fancied himself in both roles, but also wanted to play in the match. This reminded me of the selection meeting that had taken place earlier in the week.

The Badger, Hawk and I had convened on the Tuesday to pick a side to face the Wandering Has Beens. I had wanted to pick my strongest side, but The Badger believed that the match should be used as an opportunity to blood new players, or specifically player.

'No one in the other teams has really done enough

to be selected,' I had said warily, 'we already have Jez out and I am not sure who else would be good enough to play in such an important match.'

'As you know Barry we are a community club and as such we need to make sure that we include a good representation of our village,' The Badger had replied ominously, 'and so, earlier in the week over a fantastic, complimentary, lamb bhuna, I agreed with Ibrahim that his son Kamal would play.'

'Bloody hell Badg,' I had exclaimed, 'you could have at least consulted with me first. How do we know if he is any good? What does this lad Kamal even do? Bat, bowl. What?'

The Badger had looked at me, cradled his fingers and leaned back in his red chair.

'What I do know Barry, is that if Kamal does play, his father will extend the sponsorship by another year. So, I don't really care if he bats like a buffoon, bowls like, like, well like you Baz or is likelier to catch a train than the ball. He plays.'

And with that, rank had been called, and Kamal Ibrahim would make his first XI debut against a team of ex-professional cricketers this coming Saturday. Today.

So, Winners was selected in the team, leaving The Badger and injured Jez Dunstan to make unlikely event hosts. Given the extended nature of The Badger's day, Hawk had considered asking the club chair to moderate his alcohol intake but decided that a man of 70 should be able to make these decisions by himself and left it, hoping that this would not come back to haunt him later.

As all the family fun day elements were being set up efficiently under the hawkish eye of Tim Kestrel who, as noted by Flash 'looked like a 1980s bus driver' with his crimson jacket, I focused my attention on where it had been all along. And that was on the Wandering Has Beens and the on-pitch action.

I had instructed my team to turn up in full training gear at 11am for a briefing and pre-match photo with their celebrity guests, who were due to arrive at 12 noon. The Badger was going to make a welcome speech and declare the event officially open before the captains plus the mascot would walk to the middle for the pre-match toss.

They arrived in dribs and drabs, with the recently reintegrated Gordon Blackwell turning up wearing an England cricket shirt, blue cargo shorts and brown sandals with white socks, having steadfastly refused to buy any training gear, declaring it a waste of money. Instead. dressed like a middle-aged tourist looking for a bacon sandwich in Benidorm, he strolled into the bar-cum-tearoom.

'Where are they then?' he asked.

I knew that Blacky did not have the requisite pre-match apparel and so didn't point out that he was inappropriately dressed, but I did note that it was just past noon and that indeed the question posed by the WOC was accurate.

'They'll be here,' I replied anxiously and scuttled off to retrieve my phone from a protesting Ella, who had been playing a game on it. I found the number of Diana van Clutchback, who was my contact at the Wandering Has Beens and called it expectantly.

It felt like one of those times when you are expecting someone to turn up, say a plumber or a first date, and when they are one minute late you start to panic and question what they saw in you in the first place. Well maybe not the plumber.

Anyway, I digress, for as Diana's phone rang and rang, unanswered, I felt an impending sense of doom, which was heightened by twenty pairs of eyes, including those of Dave the dog, boring a hole into my already tormented soul. I had never really recovered my status with The Badger after the cheese incident and ensuing fracas and this potential non-show would see the end of me as captain.

'Well?' asked Blacky, using his words in modicum.

'Poor um reception in here, I'll go out and try,' I muttered and went outside to see if staring up the driveway of The Wreck to manifest the arrival of the celebrity opposition would yield a better outcome.

'He's cocked it up again,' said Noodle, eager to ingratiate himself with his brother, for he too hadn't recovered his position after the shirt sponsorship fiasco. Cousin Saeed had indeed delivered all three teams' shirts in good time for their matches, white shirts with the red and gold Taj Mahal Indian restaurant logo emblazoned across the front. Everyone, bar one that is, wore the shirt with pride and it was only a stern warning regarding the distribution of their aged mother's fortune that made Noodle wear his shirt the right way around.

I was worried, very worried. The bouncy castle, its towers featuring the gruesome sight of Henry VIII's late wives smiling whilst being chased by an executioner with a bloody axe, was awash with children and swaying merrily in the light breeze coming in from the west, that in turn was wafting the smells from the Taj Mahal food truck across The Wreck. Mohammed Ibrahim, the proprietor himself, noted the breeze and turned off the electric fan that had been propelling the fragrant odours to all and sundry. The chef from the Prickly Oyster, beer in hand, was firing up the BBQ, wishing that the wind was coming from the east and not blowing hickory smoke straight back into his face, and the craft ladies were chatting scones with each other, waiting for the slightest sign of interest from the growing crowd, who were being shepherded from car to bar by the efficient Jane and Louise.

All was in good order then, apart from the missing celebrities, and that was down to me.

I looked at my phone, willing it to buzz with good news from Diana, but as much as I looked, all I saw was my family smiling cheerfully back from a holiday in Margate. My lonely vigil was interrupted by a quiet voice in my ear.

'What's our Plan B mate?'

I turned, slowly, to see the concerned face of my friend, and event impresario, Tim Kestrel who put a comforting hand on my shoulder to emphasise his concern.

'They'll be here mate, don't worry, I said with

misplaced confidence.

I looked to my phone and decided to try Diana again, in the hope that even though she didn't know who had previously called, she would miraculously know this time. After three short rings, I heard the voice of an angel, albeit a posh one.

'Hello Diana van Clutchback speaking.'

'Uhh uhh h-h-hello Diana, it's B-Barry, Barry Briggs from Buntingford Smedley Cricket Club.'

'Ohh hi Barry,' she replied cheerfully, filling my heart with both joy and optimism, until she said, 'looking forward to seeing you next week.'

Silence ensued. I felt, saw, smelled, and heard my life flash before me. Daggers from Jill, my spiky mother-in-law, a lack of surprise from Jane, disappointment from Ben, rejection from the other two children, a summons by The Badger, a tearing of notes from the Hawk, howls of derision from Dazzler and a protective hug from Gilo, or maybe it was a cuff around the ear, whatever it was, it was bad, very bad.

I tried to calm myself, but failed miserably and instead wailed, 'but we agreed that it was this week. We have a Tower of London bouncy castle, craft stalls and everything.'

'Oh then it will be a lovely day for everyone,' she replied, adding to my confusion, before the cause of my misery dawned on her.

'Sorry, sorry, sorry Barry, I meant that I will see you next week. Remember, the Wandering Has Beens charity dinner that I invited you and your wife to?'

I came out of my tailspin and landed back on terra firma, the correct way up. In all the excitement I had forgotten about the dinner, but now that future event would have to take second place to the main question of where on earth the Wandering Has Beens were.

'Out of interest Barry, why did you call me?

'Because the team isn't here yet and, given the time, I wondered where they could be.' I said, with new levels of composure.

'Oh that's odd, Joe said that they were nearly there when I spoke with him at 11:45 or so. I wonder where they could have got to. I will call him and ring you back, hold tight.'

That was all that I could do and to ensure that I did indeed keep everything mentally and physically intact, I walked to the furthest corner of The Wreck, away from the restless mutterings emanating from the pavilion. It was 12:23 precisely when Diana phoned back.

'Teeny administrative cock-up, they went to Billingford instead of Buntingford, but they are on their way to you now. Joe thought that something was wrong when the wreck at Billingford was exactly that and not a cricket ground. How funny.'

With that she wished them a great day, that she would see me and my lovely wife next week to not to hesitate to call her if I needed anything else. And then she was gone.

'Need anything else,' I muttered to myself, 'what I

need is the bloody team.' But I was also grateful that Billingford was not that far away and that they should be here soon.

I looked towards the pavilion where my team was standing, in their cricket whites, arms crossed, staring at me enquiringly. Jez Dunstan fired up the music, but his choice of Dreadlock Holiday by 1970s rockers 10cc, featuring the lines I don't like cricket, I love it was not the best choice given the circumstances but just as The Badger started with a 'testing one, two' and was about to launch into a speech explaining the delay, a loud cheer erupted as the Wandering Has Beens coach turned off the main road and made its way slowly down the driveway.

I sat down on the grass, relief sweeping through my body as I saw that glorious cricketing chariot glide into view. Jill and the other naysayers would have to wait for another day before they could put me, Barry Compton Briggs down. I got up and walked smugly across the pitch and waved for my team to join me, and everyone else, to greet their celebrity guests. But when I finally reached the coach, I found myself at the back of a long queue, for at the head of the greeting party were The Badger and Mohammed Ibrahim himself.

Ex-England captain Joe Cullimore had just stepped off the coach and he was immediately accosted by the leader of the party of two.

'Colin Campbell, chair of the Buntingford Smedley Cricket Club, as well as the Conservative Club, parish council and bowling club,' said The Badger, adding 'it is indeed a rare pleasure to be in the very presence of such cricketing nobility.

'Mr. Mohammed Ibrahim also with you dearest sirs. I am the proud proprietor of the Taj Mahal Indian restaurant here in the splendid village of Buntingford Smedley as well as being the main, and only, sponsor of the cricket club.'

That was the cue for Kamal to step forward and present the World Cup winning, ex-England captain with a framed Buntingford Smedley CC shirt replete with a gold Taj Mahal logo and a two-for-one voucher at the restaurant, conditions apply.

As the rest of the stars stepped one by one off the coach, they were met by this voucher-delivering vanguard as well as the throng of children who were keen to have selfies with their heroes, even though none of them were in their sticker books. All that is except Ella, who had taken the opportunity to monopolise the bouncy castle and devise a way of benefitting financially from its next set of users.

I finally managed to make my way to Joe Cullimore.

'Hi Joe, I'm Barry, Barry Briggs, captain of the Buntingford Smedley team,' I gushed.

'Sorry we are late, we went to the wrong place,' he explained, adding 'I hope that you weren't too worried.'

'Haha no, I was calm – I knew that you were just running late,' I lied, 'but am glad that you are all here and we can get going.'

'Testing, testing one two, one two,' boomed The Badger's voice over the public announcement system. I wondered how he had managed to greet the team off the coach and still make it to the pavilion in time without breaking into a sprint.

'Most of you will know me, my name is Colin Campbell, chair of the cricket club, Conservative Club, parish council and bowling club and I am honoured to welcome Mr. Joe Cullimore, his Wandering Has Beens team and guests to the first ever family fun day here at The Wreck, Buntingford Smedley.'

'Sponsored by Taj Mahal Indian restaurant,' shouted Mohammed Ibrahim.

'Quite,' agreed The Badger

'Quiet', whispered Noodle loudly and received an elbow from his wife for his troubles.

The Badger then embarked on a thirty-minute monologue about the history of the village, the feuds, the Cholmondley-Smythes, throwing in the tale of the rumble in the fields and how the land had been bequeathed to the club, ending with a general summary of its local level successes. He said that he was proud to be associated with the club and its luminary players such as currently injured Chocks Tillwell, who had played in the county's second team and the legendary Jack Cromwell who had captained the team to their first ever league title in 1896. He did so oblivious of his audience and their own global sporting achievements.

'Get on with it Badger, we have a game to play,' came a voice from the crowd.

And with a hearty chuckle, The Badger declared the family fun day well and truly open and went off to seek a refreshing pint of beer.

I showed Joe and his team to the away changing room.

'Not quite what you are used to,' I said apologetically.

'Oh we've seen worse,' lied the ex-England captain.

I went to my own changing room and closed the door, ready to deliver my pre-match speech. However, sensing the dramatic uplift in the mood of the crowd, Jez had turned up the volume on the sound system and so whatever I had said, my team didn't hear it.

Umpire Stan Clarke, resplendent in his grey flannels, white polo shirt, navy blue bowling club blazer with club crest and a white Panama hat with a jaunty red band, for which he had caught the number 92 bus to the nearest big town and visited K. Ponsford & Sons, Purveyors of Fine Headwear since 1894, knocked on both doors and announced that it was time.

I emerged from the home changing room in my playing whites and a blazer whilst Joe, maybe not sensing the magnitude of the occasion, was wearing his Wandering Has Beens shirt, shorts and flip flops – thongs if this story ever reaches Australia. We shook hands, and I introduced Stan.

'Jolly pleased to make your acquaintance. I remember being at The Oval one year and had marvelled at your hundred versus the visitors,

West Indies I think, or was it Sri Lanka?' I always get them mixed up, but a privilege nonetheless.'

'Many thanks umpire, yes that was a great day.'

As we walked to the middle, with the crowd applauding he said 'that hundred was against India and was Joliff not me. I hope his umpiring decisions are better.'

'I wouldn't hold your breath,' I replied to my new best friend.

Because of the vast gulf in ability between a team made of up of local businesspeople, farmers and tradespeople and one consisting of ex-professional cricketers, the general rule is that the toss is ceremonial and that the amateurs are asked to bat first. There are a couple of reasons for this – firstly if the professionals batted first then they would score so many runs that the amateurs would be deflated in their attempts at a run chase and secondly if the amateurs batted first then there would be a greater chance of an early finish and more time for drinking and eating, well drinking really.

I had asked Ben to be mascot for this match and he, in matching whites and blazer, solemnly shook our hands and tossed Her Majesty into the air.

Joe called correctly and asked us to bat first as he knew the rules and, after another shake of hands and posing for The ButtPill photographer, I signalled that we were batting to prodigious cheers from both my team and the crowd.

So then, on a glorious late summer's day Flash Stevens and Gilo Aikens walked out to bat against two recently retired international bowlers from Australia and the West Indies.

The match went pretty much to script. The bowlers started off at half pace and, when they realised that some of the amateurs could bat, they cranked it up to three-quarters and occasional full whack if the batters were starting to play well. With the ball sometimes coming down at speeds over 85mph, we were bowled out for 120 in 20 overs and the batters of Wandering Has Beens had reached their target in a paltry 12 overs, with only Kamal Ibrahim coming out with any credit, having taken the wicket of the legendary Australian Trent Cobbler, who graciously congratulated the ecstatic youth to the annoyance of the WOC, G. Blackwell. When Simon Jolliff hit the winning run, the crowd erupted into cheers knowing that the real action would start and some of the younger members ran onto the pitch for selfies ad autographs with their heroes.

I congratulated my team and the opposition, walked off the pitch wearily but happy and, after a nod of approval and firm handshake from The Badger, a group photograph with the two teams and a discounted samosa from Mohammed Ibrahim himself, I walked over into the loving arms of Jane and my family.

'We're proud of you dad,' they all chimed as the sun set over the pavilion of The Wreck at Buntingford Smedley and my story.

Printed in Dunstable, United Kingdom